C# FOR WEB DEVELOPMENT

Building Dynamic Websites with

C# and ASP.NET

THOMPSON CARTER

TABLE OF CONTENTS

Introduction

The world of web development is evolving at an unprecedented pace, with technologies constantly advancing to meet the demands of modern applications. In this dynamic environment, mastering a versatile, robust, and widely adopted framework like ASP.NET Core is essential for developers aiming to create powerful, scalable, and secure web solutions. This book, *C# for Web Development: Building Dynamic Websites with C# and ASP.NET Core*, is your comprehensive guide to harnessing the full potential of C# and ASP.NET Core to build cutting-edge web applications.

Why This Book?

With the increasing demand for full-stack developers, the ability to create efficient back-end logic, coupled with an engaging and interactive front-end, has become a critical skill. ASP.NET Core, Microsoft's open-source, cross-platform framework, empowers developers to meet these demands by providing a versatile and unified development experience.

This book is designed to be:

- **Beginner-Friendly**: Whether you're just starting your journey with C# or transitioning from another programming language, this book guides you step by step through the essential concepts.

- **Comprehensive**: Covering everything from foundational programming principles to advanced topics like real-time communication, security best practices, and deployment strategies.
- **Practical**: Each chapter includes real-world examples and projects to ensure you gain hands-on experience and practical skills.

What You'll Learn

This book takes you on a journey to master C# and ASP.NET Core by systematically covering the following:

1. **Foundational Knowledge**:
    - Learn the basics of C#, including data types, control structures, object-oriented programming, and asynchronous programming.
2. **Web Development Essentials**:
    - Understand the architecture of web applications, including HTTP, MVC patterns, Razor Pages, and Blazor for building interactive UIs.
3. **Backend Development**:

- o Explore the power of ASP.NET Core for building APIs, integrating databases, and managing application state effectively.

4. **Advanced Features**:
   - o Delve into real-time communication with SignalR, advanced routing, dependency injection, and middleware development.

5. **Security Best Practices**:
   - o Protect your applications from common threats like SQL injection, XSS, and CSRF.
   - o Learn how to secure sensitive data with HTTPS, OAuth, and encryption.

6. **Performance Optimization and Scalability**:
   - o Optimize your applications for high traffic using caching, compression, and bundling.
   - o Implement scalable architectures with load balancing and auto-scaling.

7. **Deployment and Maintenance**:
   - o Prepare your application for deployment to cloud platforms like Azure and AWS.
   - o Set up CI/CD pipelines for automated testing and deployment.

Who Is This Book For?

This book is ideal for:

- **Aspiring Developers**: If you're new to web development or programming, this book provides a beginner-friendly introduction to C# and ASP.NET Core.

- **Experienced Programmers**: If you're familiar with other languages or frameworks, this book will help you transition to C# and explore its unique strengths.

- **Full-Stack Developers**: Gain a deeper understanding of how to build dynamic and interactive web applications with a unified .NET stack.

- **Students and Professionals**: Enhance your skills with hands-on projects and industry-standard practices.

How This Book Is Structured

The book is divided into 26 chapters, each focusing on a specific aspect of C# and ASP.NET Core development. Each chapter includes:

- **In-Depth Explanations**: Clear and concise descriptions of concepts.

- **Practical Examples**: Code snippets and real-world use cases.

- **Projects**: Hands-on exercises and projects to apply what you've learned.

At the end of the book, you'll find pathways for continued learning, including certification options and suggestions for advanced topics to explore.

Why C# and ASP.NET Core?

C# is a modern, versatile, and powerful programming language that has become a cornerstone of the .NET ecosystem. With its strong type system, object-oriented design, and support for functional programming, C# provides a solid foundation for building reliable applications. ASP.NET Core complements C# with its lightweight, modular, and high-performance framework for web development. Together, they offer:

- **Cross-Platform Support**: Build applications that run seamlessly on Windows, macOS, and Linux.
- **Performance and Scalability**: ASP.NET Core is one of the fastest web frameworks available today.
- **Rich Ecosystem**: Benefit from a vast array of libraries, tools, and integrations with cloud platforms.

What Awaits You

By the end of this book, you will have the knowledge and skills to:

- Build robust, scalable, and secure web applications.

- Implement industry-standard practices for development, deployment, and maintenance.
- Confidently tackle real-world challenges in modern web development.

Let's Begin

Your journey to mastering C# and ASP.NET Core starts here. Whether you aspire to build dynamic websites, real-time applications, or APIs for mobile and desktop apps, this book equips you with the tools and techniques needed to succeed in today's competitive development landscape. Let's dive in and start building something amazing!

Chapter 1: Introduction to C# for Web Development

Overview of C# and Its Role in Web Development

C# (pronounced "C-sharp") is a versatile, object-oriented programming language developed by Microsoft. It is a cornerstone of the .NET platform and is widely used for building desktop, mobile, gaming, and web applications.

1. **Why C# for Web Development?**
   - **Modern and Powerful**: Combines simplicity with robust capabilities, making it ideal for both beginners and experienced developers.
   - **Cross-Platform Development**: With .NET Core (now .NET), applications built with C# can run on Windows, macOS, and Linux.
   - **Integration with ASP.NET Core**: C# serves as the primary language for developing dynamic, scalable, and secure web applications using ASP.NET Core.

2. **C# in Web Development Ecosystem**:
   - **Back-End Logic**: Powering APIs, managing databases, and handling business logic.

o **Full-Stack Development**: Using Blazor, developers can write both client and server-side code in C#.

o **Seamless Integration**: Works effortlessly with front-end technologies like HTML, CSS, and JavaScript.

Introduction to ASP.NET Core and .NET 6/7

1. **What Is ASP.NET Core?**

   o A free, open-source framework for building modern, cloud-based, and internet-connected applications.

   o ASP.NET Core is a redesigned version of ASP.NET, built to offer greater flexibility, performance, and cross-platform support.

2. **Why Choose ASP.NET Core?**

   o **Performance**: ASP.NET Core is known for its blazing-fast performance, rivaling other popular web frameworks.

   o **Cross-Platform Support**: Develop and deploy applications on Windows, macOS, and Linux.

   o **Unified Framework**: It supports building various application types, including web apps, APIs, and microservices.

3. **.NET 6 and .NET 7 Enhancements**:

- o **Simplified Development**:
  - Minimal APIs for lightweight and faster application development.
  - Reduced boilerplate code for cleaner, more readable programs.
- o **Performance Improvements**:
  - Optimized runtime and tools for better scalability.
- o **Hot Reload**:
  - Allows developers to apply changes to running applications without restarting.

4. **Common ASP.NET Core Components**:
   - o **MVC (Model-View-Controller)**: A design pattern for creating scalable web applications.
   - o **Razor Pages**: Simplifies web UI development with page-focused coding.
   - o **Web APIs**: Enables building RESTful services for client applications.

The Benefits of Using C# for Building Modern Websites

1. **Robust Language Features**:
   - o Strongly-typed, ensuring fewer runtime errors.

- o Features like LINQ (Language Integrated Query) simplify querying data structures.

2. **Scalability**:

   - o Build applications that can grow seamlessly as user demand increases.
   - o ASP.NET Core supports horizontal scaling for handling high traffic.

3. **Security**:

   - o Out-of-the-box features like data protection, HTTPS enforcement, and authentication.
   - o Integration with identity providers like Azure AD, Google, and Facebook.

4. **Rich Ecosystem**:

   - o A vast library of tools, frameworks, and community support.
   - o NuGet packages for extending functionality without reinventing the wheel.

5. **Enterprise-Ready**:

   - o Proven track record in building mission-critical applications.
   - o Trusted by industries like finance, healthcare, and e-commerce.

Setting Up Your Development Environment

1. **Install the Required Tools**:
   - ○ **Visual Studio** (Recommended for beginners):
     - ▪ Download from Visual Studio Downloads.
     - ▪ Choose the "ASP.NET and web development" workload during installation.
   - ○ **Visual Studio Code** (Lightweight alternative):
     - ▪ Download from VS Code.
     - ▪ Install extensions for C# and .NET.

2. **Install the .NET SDK**:
   - ○ Download the latest .NET SDK (6 or 7) from Microsoft .NET.
   - ○ Verify installation:

   bash

   ```
   dotnet --version
   ```

3. **Set Up Your First Project**:
   - ○ Open a terminal or Visual Studio.
   - ○ Create a new ASP.NET Core application:

   bash

   ```
   dotnet new webapp -n MyFirstWebApp
   cd MyFirstWebApp
   dotnet run
   ```

    o   Navigate to http://localhost:5000 to see your application in action.

4. **Explore Project Structure**:

    o   **Program.cs**: Entry point of the application.

    o   **wwwroot**: Directory for static files like CSS, JavaScript, and images.

    o   **Pages** or **Controllers**: Where the application logic resides.

5. **Configure Development Environment**:

    o   Enable **Hot Reload** in Visual Studio for instant feedback.

    o   Install Git for version control and connect to GitHub for project collaboration.

In this chapter, you've gained a foundational understanding of C# and its pivotal role in web development. With its integration into ASP.NET Core, C# provides a powerful framework for creating modern, high-performing websites. Setting up your development environment is the first step in this exciting journey. As you proceed through this book, you'll delve deeper into building dynamic web applications with C# and ASP.NET Core, tackling real-world problems along the way.

Chapter 2: Understanding the Basics of C#

C# serves as the foundation for building dynamic web applications in ASP.NET Core. Before diving into advanced topics, understanding its basic syntax, control structures, and object-oriented programming (OOP) principles is crucial.

Variables, Data Types, and Operators

1. **Variables in C#**:
   - A variable is a named storage location used to store data.
   - Declaring a variable:

     csharp

     ```
     int age = 25;
     string name = "John Doe";
     ```

2. **Data Types**:
   - **Value Types**:
     - Store data directly in memory.
     - Examples: int, float, bool, char.
   - **Reference Types**:

- Store a reference to data in memory.
- Examples: string, object, arrays, and custom classes.

Common Data Types:

Data Type	Description	Example
int	Integer values	int count = 10;
float	Decimal numbers	float pi = 3.14f;
string	Text data	string name = "C#";
bool	Boolean (true/false)	bool isActive = true;

3. **Operators**:
   o **Arithmetic Operators**: +, -, *, /, %.

   csharp

   int sum = 10 + 5; // Result: 15

   o **Comparison Operators**: ==, !=, <, >, <=, >=.

   csharp

   bool isEqual = (5 == 10); // Result: false

- o **Logical Operators**: &&, ||, !.

  csharp

  ```
  bool result = (true && false);  // Result: false
  ```

Control Structures

1. **If Statements**:
   - o Used to execute code conditionally.

     csharp

     ```
     int age = 18;
     if (age >= 18)
     {
         Console.WriteLine("You are eligible to vote.");
     }
     else
     {
         Console.WriteLine("You are not eligible to vote.");
     }
     ```

2. **Loops**:
   - o Execute a block of code repeatedly.

   For Loop:

   csharp

```csharp
for (int i = 0; i < 5; i++)
{
    Console.WriteLine($"Iteration: {i}");
}
```

While Loop:

csharp

```csharp
int count = 0;
while (count < 5)
{
    Console.WriteLine($"Count: {count}");
    count++;
}
```

Do-While Loop:

csharp

```csharp
int num = 0;
do
{
    Console.WriteLine($"Number: {num}");
    num++;
} while (num < 5);
```

3. **Switch Cases**:

   o   A cleaner alternative to multiple if-else conditions.

   csharp

```
int day = 3;
switch (day)
{
  case 1:
    Console.WriteLine("Monday");
    break;
  case 2:
    Console.WriteLine("Tuesday");
    break;
  case 3:
    Console.WriteLine("Wednesday");
    break;
  default:
    Console.WriteLine("Invalid day");
    break;
}
```

Methods and Functions

1. **Defining and Calling Methods**:
   - o A method is a reusable block of code.

   csharp

   ```
   void Greet(string name)
   {
     Console.WriteLine($"Hello, {name}!");
   }
   ```

```
// Calling the method
Greet("Alice");
```

2. Return Types:

o Methods can return a value:

csharp

```csharp
int Add(int a, int b)
{
    return a + b;
}
```

```csharp
// Calling the method
int result = Add(5, 10);  // Result: 15
```

3. Parameters and Overloading:

o Methods can have multiple parameters.

o Overloading allows methods with the same name but different parameters:

csharp

```csharp
void Display(int num) { Console.WriteLine(num); }
void Display(string text) { Console.WriteLine(text); }
```

Introduction to Object-Oriented Programming (OOP) Concepts

C# is a fully object-oriented language, and OOP principles are key to writing maintainable, modular, and scalable applications.

1. **Classes and Objects**:
   - A class defines a blueprint for objects.

     csharp

     ```
     class Car
     {
         public string Make { get; set; }
         public string Model { get; set; }

         public void DisplayInfo()
         {
             Console.WriteLine($"Make: {Make}, Model: {Model}");
         }
     }

     // Creating an object
     Car car = new Car();
     car.Make = "Toyota";
     car.Model = "Corolla";
     car.DisplayInfo();
     ```

2. **Encapsulation**:
   - Restricts direct access to class members, exposing them through properties or methods.

     csharp

```csharp
class Account
{
    private double balance;

    public void Deposit(double amount)
    {
        balance += amount;
    }

    public double GetBalance()
    {
        return balance;
    }
}

Account account = new Account();
account.Deposit(500);
Console.WriteLine(account.GetBalance());
```

3. **Inheritance**:

   o Enables a class to inherit members from another class.

   csharp

```csharp
class Vehicle
{
    public string Type { get; set; }
}
```

```
class Bike : Vehicle
{
    public string Brand { get; set; }
}
```

```
Bike bike = new Bike { Type = "Two-Wheeler", Brand =
"Yamaha" };
Console.WriteLine($"{bike.Brand} is a {bike.Type}");
```

4. **Polymorphism**:

o Allows a method to behave differently based on the context.

csharp

```
class Shape
{
    public virtual void Draw() { Console.WriteLine("Drawing a
shape."); }
}
```

```
class Circle : Shape
{
    public override void Draw() { Console.WriteLine("Drawing
a circle."); }
}
```

```
Shape shape = new Circle();
shape.Draw(); // Output: Drawing a circle.
```

5. **Abstraction**:

   o Hides implementation details and exposes functionality through abstract classes or interfaces.

   csharp

   ```csharp
   abstract class Animal
   {
       public abstract void Speak();
   }

   class Dog : Animal
   {
       public override void Speak() { Console.WriteLine("Bark!");
   }
   }

   Animal animal = new Dog();
   animal.Speak();
   ```

This chapter provided a foundational understanding of C#, covering variables, control structures, methods, and OOP concepts. These fundamentals are the building blocks for developing dynamic web applications in ASP.NET Core. In the next chapter, we'll explore the basics of web development, bridging the gap between C# programming and creating interactive web applications.

Chapter 3: Fundamentals of Web Development

Web development is the backbone of the modern internet. In this chapter, we'll explore what web development entails, its key technologies, and how server-side languages like C# fit into the ecosystem. By the end, you'll create your first simple website.

What is Web Development?

Web development is the process of building, maintaining, and optimizing websites or web applications. It involves three main areas:

1. **Frontend Development**:
   - Focuses on the user interface (UI) and user experience (UX).
   - Technologies include HTML, CSS, and JavaScript.
2. **Backend Development**:
   - Handles server-side logic, database management, and API integrations.
   - Technologies include C#, Python, Node.js, and Java.
3. **Full-Stack Development**:
   - Combines both frontend and backend development.

o A full-stack developer builds the entire web application, from server-side functionality to client-facing interfaces.

Web Development in Practice:

- Common applications include e-commerce websites, content management systems, and social networking platforms.

HTTP, HTML, CSS, and JavaScript: A Quick Overview

1. **HTTP (Hypertext Transfer Protocol)**:
    o A protocol for transferring data between a client (browser) and a server.
    o **HTTP Request**:
        - Sent by the browser to the server (e.g., a request for a webpage).
    o **HTTP Response**:
        - Sent by the server to the browser, often containing HTML, CSS, or JavaScript.
2. **HTML (HyperText Markup Language)**:
    o Defines the structure of a webpage.
    o Example:

html

```
<!DOCTYPE html>
<html>
<head>
  <title>My First Webpage</title>
</head>
<body>
  <h1>Welcome to My Website</h1>
  <p>This is a simple paragraph.</p>
</body>
</html>
```

3. **CSS (Cascading Style Sheets)**:

    o   Styles the HTML content, controlling layout, colors, and fonts.

    o   Example:

    html

```
<style>
  body {
    background-color: lightblue;
    font-family: Arial, sans-serif;
  }
  h1 {
    color: navy;
  }
</style>
```

4. **JavaScript**:

   o Adds interactivity to a website (e.g., form validation, dynamic content updates).

   o Example:

   html

   ```
   <script>
     function greet() {
       alert('Welcome to my website!');
     }
   </script>
   <button onclick="greet()">Click Me</button>
   ```

The Role of Server-Side Languages Like C#

While HTML, CSS, and JavaScript handle the client-side, server-side languages like C# power the backend of a web application. Their primary roles include:

1. **Dynamic Content Generation**:

   o C# creates HTML dynamically based on user input or database queries.

   o Example: Displaying personalized greetings based on the user's name.

2. **Business Logic Implementation**:

   o Processes complex calculations, data manipulations, and decision-making logic.

3. **Database Interactions**:

   o C# uses libraries like Entity Framework to fetch and update data in databases.

4. **Security**:

   o Handles authentication, encryption, and access control to ensure secure interactions.

5. **API Creation**:

   o C# builds RESTful APIs for mobile apps, client-side JavaScript, and third-party integrations.

Building Your First Simple Website

Let's create a basic website using ASP.NET Core with C#. This example demonstrates the integration of backend logic with frontend technologies.

Step 1: Create an ASP.NET Core Project

1. Open Visual Studio or a terminal.
2. Run the following command to create a new ASP.NET Core web application:

bash

```
dotnet new webapp -n MyFirstWebsite
cd MyFirstWebsite
```

3. Start the application:

bash

dotnet run

4. Open http://localhost:5000 in a browser to view your basic website.

Step 2: Modify the HTML Structure

1. Navigate to the Pages folder and open Index.cshtml.
2. Replace the content with:

html

```
@page
<!DOCTYPE html>
<html>
<head>
    <title>Welcome to My First Website</title>
    <style>
      body {
        font-family: Arial, sans-serif;
        text-align: center;
        margin-top: 50px;
      }
      h1 {
        color: navy;
```

```
    }
  </style>
</head>
<body>
  <h1>Hello, World!</h1>
  <p>This is my first web application built with ASP.NET Core and
C#.</p>
</body>
</html>
```

Step 3: Add Dynamic Content with C#

1. Open Index.cshtml.cs and add a property:

   csharp

   ```csharp
   public class IndexModel : PageModel
   {
       public string CurrentTime { get; private set; }

       public void OnGet()
       {
           CurrentTime = DateTime.Now.ToString("hh:mm:ss tt");
       }
   }
   ```

2. Update Index.cshtml to display the dynamic content:

   html

```
<body>
  <h1>Hello, World!</h1>
  <p>The current time is: @Model.CurrentTime</p>
</body>
```

Step 4: Run and View Your Website

- Restart your application using dotnet run.
- Refresh the browser to see your dynamic website, which displays the current time.

In this chapter, we explored the fundamentals of web development, including HTTP, HTML, CSS, and JavaScript. We also discussed how server-side languages like C# power the backend of modern web applications. By creating your first simple website with ASP.NET Core, you've taken the first step toward building dynamic, feature-rich web applications. In the next chapter, we'll dive deeper into ASP.NET Core and learn about its MVC architecture.

Chapter 4: Introduction to ASP.NET Core

ASP.NET Core is a powerful framework for building modern, scalable, and cross-platform web applications. This chapter introduces the MVC pattern, guides you through setting up an ASP.NET Core project, and helps you create your first application using Razor Pages and views.

Understanding the MVC (Model-View-Controller) Pattern

The **Model-View-Controller (MVC)** pattern is a design paradigm that separates an application into three interconnected components:

1. **Model**:
   - Represents the application's data and business logic.
   - Handles data retrieval, storage, and updates.
   - Example: A Product class with properties like Name, Price, and Description.

2. **View**:
   - Defines how the data is presented to the user.
   - Typically HTML pages with embedded Razor syntax (.cshtml files).
   - Example: A page that displays a product catalog.

3. **Controller**:

- o Manages user input, processes it, and determines the data to send to the view.
- o Acts as a mediator between the Model and the View.
- o Example: A ProductController that retrieves products from the database and passes them to the view.

How MVC Works:

- **User Request**: The user sends a request (e.g., clicking a link).
- **Controller Action**: The controller processes the request and interacts with the model if necessary.
- **View Rendering**: The controller returns a view, which is rendered and sent back to the user.

Setting Up an ASP.NET Core Project

1. **Install Required Tools**:
   - o **.NET SDK**: Download from Microsoft .NET.
   - o **Visual Studio** (or Visual Studio Code): Install the ASP.NET and web development workload.

2. **Create a New Project**:
   - o Open Visual Studio or a terminal and create a new ASP.NET Core MVC project:

   bash

```
dotnet new mvc -n MyFirstMVCApp
cd MyFirstMVCApp
```

3. **Understand the Project Structure**:

   o **Controllers**: Handles incoming requests (e.g., HomeController.cs).

   o **Models**: Represents the application's data.

   o **Views**: Defines the user interface (e.g., Index.cshtml).

4. **Run the Project**:

   o Start the application:

   bash

   dotnet run

   o Open http://localhost:5000 to view the default ASP.NET Core MVC application.

Creating Your First ASP.NET Core Application

Step 1: Add a New Controller

1. In the Controllers folder, create a new file named ProductController.cs:

   csharp

   using Microsoft.AspNetCore.Mvc;

```
public class ProductController : Controller
{
    public IActionResult Index()
    {
        ViewData["Message"] = "Welcome to the Product Page!";
        return View();
    }
}
```

2. **Explanation**:

   o Index is an action method that returns a view.

   o ViewData is used to pass data from the controller to the view.

Step 2: Add a Corresponding View

1. In the Views folder, create a new folder named Product.
2. Inside the Product folder, create a new file named Index.cshtml:

html

```
@page
@model dynamic
<!DOCTYPE html>
<html>
<head>
    <title>Product Page</title>
```

```
</head>
<body>
  <h1>@ViewData["Message"]</h1>
</body>
</html>
```

3. **Run the Application**:

   o Navigate to http://localhost:5000/Product in your browser to see the custom Product page.

Overview of Razor Pages and Views

1. **What Are Razor Pages?**

   o Razor Pages are a simpler way to build page-focused web applications in ASP.NET Core.

   o Each Razor Page consists of:

      ▪ A .cshtml file for the UI.

      ▪ A .cshtml.cs file for the page's logic.

Example:

   o File: Pages/About.cshtml

   html

   ```
   @page
   <!DOCTYPE html>
   ```

```
<html>
<head>
  <title>About</title>
</head>
<body>
  <h1>About Us</h1>
  <p>This is a sample Razor page.</p>
</body>
</html>
```

2. **Views in MVC**:

   o   Views are used in the MVC pattern to render user interfaces.

   o   Razor syntax allows mixing HTML with C# logic.

   html

```
@foreach (var product in Model.Products)
{
    <p>@product.Name - $@product.Price</p>
}
```

3. **Comparing Razor Pages and Views**:

Feature	Razor Pages	Views in MVC
Use Case	Page-specific logic (e.g., About page).	Shared logic across views (e.g., layouts).

Feature	Razor Pages	Views in MVC
Complexity	Simpler and more focused.	Suitable for larger applications.
Structure	Self-contained (.cshtml + .cshtml.cs).	Separate controllers and models.

In this chapter, we explored the fundamentals of ASP.NET Core, focusing on the MVC pattern, project setup, and the roles of Razor Pages and views. You also created your first ASP.NET Core application, learning how controllers, models, and views work together to build dynamic websites. In the next chapter, we'll dive deeper into models and data handling in ASP.NET Core, including data validation and binding.

Chapter 5: Working with Models and Data

Models are at the core of ASP.NET Core applications, representing the data and business logic. In this chapter, you'll learn how to define and use models, bind them to views, and validate data using annotations.

Introduction to Models in ASP.NET Core

1. **What Are Models?**
   - Models are classes that represent the data and logic of an application.
   - They serve as the intermediary between the database and the user interface.
   - Example: A Product model might contain properties like Name, Price, and Category.

2. **Role of Models**:
   - Define the structure of data.
   - Enforce business rules and validations.
   - Interact with data storage mechanisms (e.g., databases).

3. **Types of Models in ASP.NET Core**:

- o **View Models**: Tailored for passing data between controllers and views.
- o **Domain Models**: Represent business entities in the application.
- o **Data Transfer Objects (DTOs)**: Simplified models for transferring data between layers or APIs.

Defining and Working with Classes

1. **Creating a Model Class**:
   - o Example: Product model.

   csharp

   ```csharp
   public class Product
   {
       public int Id { get; set; }
       public string Name { get; set; }
       public decimal Price { get; set; }
       public string Category { get; set; }
   }
   ```

   - o **Explanation**:
     - Id: A unique identifier for each product.
     - Name, Price, Category: Properties to store product details.

2. Using Models in a Controller:

- Example: ProductController with sample data.

csharp

```
public class ProductController : Controller
{
    public IActionResult Index()
    {
        var products = new List<Product>
        {
            new Product { Id = 1, Name = "Laptop", Price = 999.99M, Category = "Electronics" },
            new Product { Id = 2, Name = "Chair", Price = 49.99M, Category = "Furniture" }
        };

        return View(products);
    }
}
```

Binding Models to Views

1. Passing Data from Controller to View:

- The Index method in the controller returns a list of products.
- The view displays the list.

2. Creating a Strongly-Typed View:

o   In the Views/Product folder, create Index.cshtml:

html

```
@model IEnumerable<Product>

<!DOCTYPE html>
<html>
<head>
  <title>Product List</title>
</head>
<body>
  <h1>Product List</h1>
  <table border="1">
    <thead>
      <tr>
        <th>Id</th>
        <th>Name</th>
        <th>Price</th>
        <th>Category</th>
      </tr>
    </thead>
    <tbody>
      @foreach (var product in Model)
      {
        <tr>
          <td>@product.Id</td>
          <td>@product.Name</td>
          <td>@product.Price</td>
          <td>@product.Category</td>
```

```
            </tr>
        }
    </tbody>
</table>
</body>
</html>
```

- o **Explanation**:
  - ▪ @model IEnumerable<Product>: Binds the view to a list of Product objects.
  - ▪ foreach: Iterates through the list to render each product.

Data Validation and Annotations

1. **What Are Data Annotations?**
   - o Data annotations are attributes applied to model properties to enforce rules and validations.
2. **Common Data Annotations**:

Attribute	Purpose	Example
[Required]	Ensures the field is	[Required] public string Name { get; set; }

Attribute	Purpose	Example
	not null or empty.	
[StringLength(x)]	Limits the length of a string.	[StringLength(50)] public string Name { get; set; }
[Range(x, y)]	Validates a numeric range.	[Range(1, 100)] public int Quantity { get; set; }
[DataType(DataType.EmailAddress)]	Validates email format.	[DataType(DataType.EmailAddress)] public string Email { get; set; }

3. **Adding Validation to a Model**:
   o Updated Product model with annotations:

csharp

```csharp
public class Product
{
    public int Id { get; set; }

    [Required]
    [StringLength(100)]
    public string Name { get; set; }

    [Range(0.01, 10000.00)]
    public decimal Price { get; set; }

    [Required]
    public string Category { get; set; }
}
```

4. **Displaying Validation Errors in Views**:

   o   Add a form for creating a new product:

   html

```html
@model Product

<form method="post" asp-action="Create">
  <div>
    <label>Name:</label>
    <input asp-for="Name" />
    <span asp-validation-for="Name"></span>
  </div>
```

```html
<div>
  <label>Price:</label>
  <input asp-for="Price" />
  <span asp-validation-for="Price"></span>
</div>
<div>
  <label>Category:</label>
  <input asp-for="Category" />
  <span asp-validation-for="Category"></span>
</div>
<button type="submit">Create</button>
</form>

<script
src="https://cdnjs.cloudflare.com/ajax/libs/jquery/3.6.0/jquery.
min.js"></script>
<script                    src="https://cdn.jsdelivr.net/npm/jquery-
validation/dist/jquery.validate.min.js"></script>
<script    src="https://cdn.jsdelivr.net/npm/jquery-validation-
unobtrusive/dist/jquery.validate.unobtrusive.min.js"></script>
```

- **Explanation**:
  - asp-for binds the input fields to model properties.
  - asp-validation-for displays validation errors.

5. **Controller Action for Validation**:
   - Example Create method in ProductController:

   csharp

```
[HttpPost]
public IActionResult Create(Product product)
{
    if (ModelState.IsValid)
    {
        // Save product to the database
        return RedirectToAction("Index");
    }

    return View(product);
}
```

In this chapter, we explored the fundamentals of working with models in ASP.NET Core. You learned how to define model classes, bind them to views, and enforce data validation using annotations. These concepts are vital for managing application data and ensuring robust user interactions. In the next chapter, we'll delve deeper into controllers and routing to understand how requests are handled in ASP.NET Core.

Chapter 6: Controllers and Routing

In ASP.NET Core, **controllers** are responsible for handling user requests and directing the application's behavior. **Routing** defines how these requests are mapped to specific controllers and their actions. In this chapter, you'll learn to create and manage controllers, understand routing, and build custom routes. Finally, we'll create a simple blog application to tie these concepts together.

Creating and Managing Controllers

1. **What Are Controllers?**
   - Controllers are classes that handle HTTP requests, process data (via models), and return responses (e.g., views, JSON, or plain text).
   - In ASP.NET Core MVC, controllers inherit from the Controller base class.

2. **Creating a Controller**:
   - Example: Create a BlogController to handle blog-related functionality.

     csharp

     using Microsoft.AspNetCore.Mvc;

     public class BlogController : Controller

```csharp
{
    public IActionResult Index()
    {
        return View();
    }

    public IActionResult Details(int id)
    {
        return Content($"Blog post ID: {id}");
    }
}
```

3. **Controller Methods (Actions)**:
   - **Action Methods**:
     - Respond to HTTP requests.
     - Return a result (e.g., View(), Json(), Content()).
   - Example:

   csharp

```csharp
public IActionResult About()
{
    return Content("This is a simple blog application.");
}
```

4. **Types of Results**:
   - ViewResult: Returns a view to the client.
   - JsonResult: Returns JSON data (useful for APIs).
   - ContentResult: Returns raw content as a string.

o RedirectResult: Redirects to another URL or action.

Understanding Routing in ASP.NET Core

1. **What Is Routing?**

   o Routing determines how an HTTP request maps to a controller action.

   o ASP.NET Core uses attribute-based or convention-based routing.

2. **Default Routing**:

   o The default route is defined in Program.cs or Startup.cs (depending on the project setup):

   csharp

```
app.MapControllerRoute(
    name: "default",
    pattern: "{controller=Home}/{action=Index}/{id?}");
```

   o **Pattern Explanation**:

      ▪ {controller}: Specifies the controller name (e.g., BlogController).

      ▪ {action}: Specifies the action method (e.g., Index).

      ▪ {id?}: Optional route parameter.

3. **Attribute Routing**:

- o Attribute routing maps URLs to actions using attributes.
- o Example:

csharp

```csharp
[Route("blog")]
public class BlogController : Controller
{
    [Route("")]
    public IActionResult Index()
    {
        return View();
    }

    [Route("{id:int}")]
    public IActionResult Details(int id)
    {
        return Content($"Viewing blog post ID: {id}");
    }
}
```

Building Custom Routes

1. **Customizing Route Patterns**:
   - o Routes can include constraints and default values.
   - o Example:

csharp

```
app.MapControllerRoute(
    name: "blog",
    pattern: "blog/{id:int}",
    defaults: new { controller = "Blog", action = "Details" });
```

2. **Route Constraints**:

- o Enforce specific patterns for parameters:

Constraint	Example	Description
{id:int}	/blog/123	Matches integers only.
{slug:alpha}	/blog/tech	Matches alphabetic strings.
{date:datetime}	/blog/2025-01-01	Matches date/time format.

3. **Custom Route Attributes**:

- o Example: Define a custom route for blog categories.

csharp

```
[Route("blog/category/{category}")]
public IActionResult Category(string category)
{
    return Content($"Category: {category}");
}
```

Real-World Example: Building a Simple Blog Application

Objective: Create a basic blog application with controllers, routing, and views.

Step 1: Create the Model

- Define a BlogPost model:

csharp

```
public class BlogPost
{
    public int Id { get; set; }
    public string Title { get; set; }
    public string Content { get; set; }
    public DateTime PublishedDate { get; set; }
}
```

Step 2: Create the Controller

- Define a BlogController with some sample data:

csharp

```
public class BlogController : Controller
{
```

```csharp
private static List<BlogPost> _posts = new List<BlogPost>
{
    new BlogPost { Id = 1, Title = "First Post", Content = "Hello,
world!", PublishedDate = DateTime.Now },
    new BlogPost { Id = 2, Title = "ASP.NET Core Tips", Content =
"Learn MVC and Razor Pages.", PublishedDate = DateTime.Now }
};

[Route("blog")]
public IActionResult Index()
{
    return View(_posts);
}

[Route("blog/{id:int}")]
public IActionResult Details(int id)
{
    var post = _posts.FirstOrDefault(p => p.Id == id);
    if (post == null) return NotFound();
    return View(post);
}
}
```

Step 3: Create Views

1. **Index View**:
    o **File:** Views/Blog/Index.cshtml

    html

```
@model IEnumerable<BlogPost>

<h1>Blog Posts</h1>
<ul>
    @foreach (var post in Model)
    {
       <li>
          <a     href="/blog/@post.Id">@post.Title</a>     -
@post.PublishedDate.ToShortDateString()
       </li>
    }
</ul>
```

2. **Details View**:

   o **File:** Views/Blog/Details.cshtml

   html

```
@model BlogPost

<h1>@Model.Title</h1>
<p><strong>Published:</strong> @Model.PublishedDate</p>
<p>@Model.Content</p>
<a href="/blog">Back to Blog</a>
```

Step 4: Test the Application

- Run the application using dotnet run.

- Navigate to:
    - /blog: Lists all blog posts.
    - /blog/1: Displays the details of the first blog post.

In this chapter, you've learned the essentials of controllers and routing in ASP.NET Core. You explored how to create controllers, manage routes, and build custom route patterns. The real-world example of a simple blog application demonstrated how these elements work together to create a functional web application. In the next chapter, we'll delve into Razor Pages to simplify page-based development.

Chapter 7: Understanding Razor Pages

Razor Pages in ASP.NET Core provide a simpler, page-focused programming model that combines the power of Razor syntax with the structure of ASP.NET Core. This chapter introduces Razor syntax, demonstrates how to use Razor Pages to create dynamic web pages, and walks you through building a real-world product catalog.

Razor Syntax and Its Advantages

1. **What Is Razor Syntax?**
   - Razor is a lightweight markup syntax for embedding server-side C# code into HTML.
   - It uses the @ symbol to transition between HTML and C#.

   Example:

   html

   <h1>Hello, @UserName!</h1>

2. **Key Features of Razor Syntax**:
   - **Inline C# Code**:
     - You can write C# directly in HTML.

     html

```
<p>The current time is: @DateTime.Now</p>
```

- o **Loops and Conditionals**:
  - ▪ Use @ to include control structures like loops and conditionals.

  html

  ```
  @if (DateTime.Now.Hour < 12)
  {
      <p>Good morning!</p>
  }
  else
  {
      <p>Good afternoon!</p>
  }
  ```

3. **Advantages of Razor Syntax**:
   - o Simplifies server-side code integration with HTML.
   - o Offers seamless data binding.
   - o Reduces complexity compared to traditional ASP.NET Web Forms.

Using Razor Pages in ASP.NET Core

1. **What Are Razor Pages?**

- o Razor Pages are a page-focused programming model in ASP.NET Core.
- o Each Razor Page consists of:
  - A .cshtml file (HTML markup and Razor code).
  - A .cshtml.cs file (C# code-behind logic).

2. **Setting Up Razor Pages**:
   - o **Enable Razor Pages** in your project: Ensure your project is configured for Razor Pages in Program.cs:

csharp

```
app.MapRazorPages();
```

3. **Creating Razor Pages**:
   - o Add a Razor Page to the Pages directory.
   - o Example: Create a Products page.
     - **Products.cshtml**:

html

```
@page
@model ProductsModel

<h1>Product List</h1>
<ul>
    @foreach (var product in Model.Products)
    {
```

```
        <li>@product</li>
    }
</ul>
```

- **Products.cshtml.cs**:

csharp

using Microsoft.AspNetCore.Mvc.RazorPages;

```csharp
public class ProductsModel : PageModel
{
    public List<string> Products { get; set; }

    public void OnGet()
    {
        Products = new List<string> { "Laptop",
"Phone", "Tablet" };
    }
}
```

4. **Routing in Razor Pages**:

   o Razor Pages use file-based routing, where the URL corresponds to the page file's path.

   - Example: Pages/Products.cshtml maps to /Products.

Creating Dynamic Web Pages

Dynamic web pages allow content to change based on user input or data from a backend source.

1. **Data Binding in Razor Pages**:
   - Bind data from the PageModel to the .cshtml file using properties.
   - Example:

   html

   ```
   <p>Welcome, @Model.UserName!</p>
   ```

2. **Handling Form Input**:
   - Razor Pages make form handling simple with the OnPost method.
     - Example: Capturing user input from a form.
       - **HTML**:

       html

       ```
       <form method="post">
           <label for="name">Enter your name:</label>
           <input id="name" name="UserName" />
           <button type="submit">Submit</button>
       </form>
       <p>Hello, @Model.UserName!</p>
       ```

       - **Code-Behind**:

csharp

```csharp
public class GreetingModel : PageModel
{
    [BindProperty]
    public string UserName { get; set; }

    public void OnPost()
    {
        // Process user input
    }
}
```

3. **Interacting with Databases**:
   - Use Entity Framework Core to fetch data for Razor Pages dynamically.
   - Example: Fetching a list of products from a database.

Real-World Example: Building a Dynamic Product Catalog

Objective: Create a product catalog that dynamically displays product details and allows users to search for products.

Step 1: Set Up the Model

1. Create a Product class:

csharp

```
public class Product
{
    public int Id { get; set; }
    public string Name { get; set; }
    public decimal Price { get; set; }
    public string Description { get; set; }
}
```

Step 2: Configure the PageModel

1. Add a CatalogModel class in the Pages folder:

csharp

```
public class CatalogModel : PageModel
{
    public List<Product> Products { get; set; }

    public void OnGet()
    {
        Products = new List<Product>
        {
            new Product { Id = 1, Name = "Laptop", Price = 999.99M,
Description = "High-performance laptop" },
            new Product { Id = 2, Name = "Smartphone", Price = 499.99M,
Description = "Latest Android smartphone" }
        };
```

```
        }
    }
```

Step 3: Design the Razor Page

1. Create a Catalog.cshtml file:

    html

    ```
    @page
    @model CatalogModel

    <h1>Product Catalog</h1>
    <table border="1">
      <thead>
        <tr>
          <th>Name</th>
          <th>Price</th>
          <th>Description</th>
        </tr>
      </thead>
      <tbody>
        @foreach (var product in Model.Products)
        {
          <tr>
            <td>@product.Name</td>
            <td>@product.Price.ToString("C")</td>
            <td>@product.Description</td>
          </tr>
    ```

```
        }
    </tbody>
</table>
```

Step 4: Add Search Functionality

1. Update the CatalogModel to include search functionality:

csharp

```csharp
public class CatalogModel : PageModel
{
    public List<Product> Products { get; set; }
    public string SearchTerm { get; set; }

    public void OnGet(string searchTerm)
    {
        Products = new List<Product>
        {
            new Product { Id = 1, Name = "Laptop", Price = 999.99M,
Description = "High-performance laptop" },
            new Product { Id = 2, Name = "Smartphone", Price = 499.99M,
Description = "Latest Android smartphone" }
        };

        if (!string.IsNullOrEmpty(searchTerm))
        {
            Products = Products.Where(p => p.Name.Contains(searchTerm,
StringComparison.OrdinalIgnoreCase)).ToList();
```

```
        }
      }
   }
```

2. Update Catalog.cshtml with a search form:

html

```html
<form method="get">
  <label for="search">Search Products:</label>
  <input              id="search"              name="searchTerm"
value="@Model.SearchTerm" />
  <button type="submit">Search</button>
</form>
```

In this chapter, you learned the fundamentals of Razor Pages, including their structure, syntax, and use in creating dynamic web pages. The real-world example of a dynamic product catalog demonstrated how Razor Pages simplify data-driven development while offering robust features. In the next chapter, we'll explore forms and data binding in detail, focusing on user input and validation.

Chapter 8: Forms and Data Binding

Forms are essential in web applications, enabling user input for tasks like registration, login, and data submission. ASP.NET Core simplifies form creation, data binding, and validation, making user interaction intuitive and efficient. In this chapter, you'll learn how to create and process forms, understand data binding, and validate user input. You'll also build a real-world user registration form.

Creating and Processing Forms

1. **What Are Forms?**
   - Forms are used to collect user input and send it to the server for processing.
   - In ASP.NET Core, forms can be created using Razor Pages or MVC Views with Razor syntax.
2. **Creating a Basic Form**:
   - Example: A simple form to capture a user's name.
     - **HTML Form**:

     html

     ```
     <form method="post" asp-page="/Welcome">
         <label for="name">Enter your name:</label>
         <input id="name" name="UserName" />
         <button type="submit">Submit</button>
     ```

```
</form>
```

- **Processing the Form**:
  - Create a Welcome Razor Page with the OnPost method to process the input.

    csharp

    ```csharp
    public class WelcomeModel : PageModel
    {
      [BindProperty]
      public string UserName { get; set; }

      public void OnPost()
      {
        ViewData["Message"]        =        $"Hello,
    {UserName}!";
      }
    }
    ```

  - **Display the Result**:

    html

    ```html
    <h1>@ViewData["Message"]</h1>
    ```

3. **Form Attributes**:
   - method: Specifies the HTTP method (GET or POST).
   - action: Defines the URL where the form is submitted.

o   asp-page or asp-action: Specifies the Razor Page or MVC action to handle the request.

Understanding Data Binding in ASP.NET Core

1. **What Is Data Binding?**
   - o Data binding connects form inputs to model properties or controller parameters.
   - o In Razor Pages, the BindProperty attribute automates data binding.

2. **Binding with Razor Pages**:
   - o Example:

   csharp

   ```csharp
   public class RegistrationModel : PageModel
   {
     [BindProperty]
     public string FirstName { get; set; }

     public void OnPost()
     {
       // FirstName is automatically bound to the form input
     }
   }
   ```

   - ▪ **Form**:

html

```
<form method="post">
  <label for="firstname">First Name:</label>
  <input id="firstname" asp-for="FirstName" />
  <button type="submit">Submit</button>
</form>
```

3. **Model Binding in MVC**:

   o In MVC, parameters in controller actions are automatically bound to form fields.

   o Example:

   csharp

```
public IActionResult Register(string firstName)
{
    // firstName is bound to the form input
    return Content($"Welcome, {firstName}!");
}
```

Validating User Input

1. **Introduction to Validation**:

   o Validation ensures that user input meets specific requirements before processing.

   o ASP.NET Core supports both server-side and client-side validation.

2. **Using Data Annotations**:

   o Data annotations are attributes applied to model properties for validation.

   o Example:

   csharp

```csharp
public class User
{
    [Required]
    public string Name { get; set; }

    [EmailAddress]
    public string Email { get; set; }

    [Range(18, 120)]
    public int Age { get; set; }
}
```

3. **Displaying Validation Errors in Forms**:

   o Use the asp-validation-for tag helper to display validation messages.

   o Example:

   html

```html
<form method="post">
    <label for="name">Name:</label>
    <input id="name" asp-for="Name" />
```

```
<span asp-validation-for="Name"></span>

<label for="email">Email:</label>
<input id="email" asp-for="Email" />
<span asp-validation-for="Email"></span>

<button type="submit">Submit</button>
</form>
```

4. **Enabling Client-Side Validation**:

   o Include validation libraries in the layout file:

   html

   ```
   <script
   src="https://cdnjs.cloudflare.com/ajax/libs/jquery/3.6.0/jquery.
   min.js"></script>
   <script              src="https://cdn.jsdelivr.net/npm/jquery-
   validation/dist/jquery.validate.min.js"></script>
   <script    src="https://cdn.jsdelivr.net/npm/jquery-validation-
   unobtrusive/dist/jquery.validate.unobtrusive.min.js"></script>
   ```

Real-World Example: Building a User Registration Form

Objective: Create a user registration form that collects and validates user details, such as name, email, and password.

Step 1: Create the Model

- Define a User class for registration data:

csharp

```csharp
public class User
{
    [Required]
    [StringLength(50)]
    public string Name { get; set; }

    [Required]
    [EmailAddress]
    public string Email { get; set; }

    [Required]
    [StringLength(100, MinimumLength = 6)]
    [DataType(DataType.Password)]
    public string Password { get; set; }
}
```

Step 2: Create the PageModel

- Define a RegisterModel class:

csharp

```csharp
public class RegisterModel : PageModel
{
    [BindProperty]
```

```
public User User { get; set; }

public void OnPost()
{
    if (!ModelState.IsValid)
    {
        // Handle invalid input
        return;
    }

    // Save user data to the database (mocked here)
    ViewData["Message"] = $"User {User.Name} registered
successfully!";
    }
}
```

Step 3: Design the Razor Page

- Create a Register.cshtml file:

html

```
@page
@model RegisterModel

<h1>User Registration</h1>

<form method="post">
    <div>
```

```html
        <label for="name">Name:</label>
        <input id="name" asp-for="User.Name" />
        <span asp-validation-for="User.Name"></span>
    </div>

    <div>
        <label for="email">Email:</label>
        <input id="email" asp-for="User.Email" />
        <span asp-validation-for="User.Email"></span>
    </div>

    <div>
        <label for="password">Password:</label>
        <input id="password" asp-for="User.Password" />
        <span asp-validation-for="User.Password"></span>
    </div>

    <button type="submit">Register</button>
</form>

@if (ViewData["Message"] != null)
{
    <p>@ViewData["Message"]</p>
}

<script
src="https://cdnjs.cloudflare.com/ajax/libs/jquery/3.6.0/jquery.min.js">
</script>
<script                         src="https://cdn.jsdelivr.net/npm/jquery-
validation/dist/jquery.validate.min.js"></script>
```

```
<script            src="https://cdn.jsdelivr.net/npm/jquery-validation-
unobtrusive/dist/jquery.validate.unobtrusive.min.js"></script>
```

Step 4: Test the Application

1. Run the application using dotnet run.
2. Navigate to /Register to access the registration form.
3. Test the form with valid and invalid input to see how validation works.

This chapter covered the fundamentals of creating and processing forms, data binding in ASP.NET Core, and validating user input using data annotations. The real-world example of a user registration form demonstrated how to create dynamic, interactive, and secure web pages. In the next chapter, we'll explore working with databases and integrating them into your web application.

Chapter 9: Working with Databases

Databases are an essential part of most web applications, storing and retrieving data for dynamic functionality. ASP.NET Core integrates seamlessly with **Entity Framework Core (EF Core),** a powerful object-relational mapper (ORM) that simplifies database interactions. In this chapter, you'll learn about EF Core, set up a database, perform CRUD operations, and build a real-world task management system.

Introduction to Entity Framework Core

1. **What Is EF Core?**
   - EF Core is an open-source, lightweight, and extensible ORM for .NET.
   - It provides a high-level API to interact with databases using C# objects, eliminating the need for raw SQL queries.
2. **Key Features**:
   - **Code-First Approach**: Define database schema using C# classes.
   - **Migrations**: Evolve your database schema as the application changes.

- o **LINQ Integration**: Query the database using LINQ (Language Integrated Query).

3. **Supported Databases**:
   - o SQL Server, PostgreSQL, MySQL, SQLite, and more.

4. **Why Use EF Core?**
   - o Simplifies data access code.
   - o Maintains a strong relationship between database and application logic.
   - o Supports advanced features like lazy loading and change tracking.

Setting Up a Database for Your Application

1. **Install EF Core Packages**:
   - o Add EF Core to your project:

   bash

   ```
   dotnet add package Microsoft.EntityFrameworkCore
   dotnet add package Microsoft.EntityFrameworkCore.SqlServer
   dotnet add package Microsoft.EntityFrameworkCore.Tools
   ```

2. **Define the Database Context**:
   - o The DbContext class represents a session with the database and allows CRUD operations.

o Example: Create AppDbContext:

csharp

```
using Microsoft.EntityFrameworkCore;

public class AppDbContext : DbContext
{
    public DbSet<TaskItem> TaskItems { get; set; }

    protected                override                void
OnConfiguring(DbContextOptionsBuilder options)
    {
        options.UseSqlServer("YourConnectionString");
    }
}
```

3. **Define the Model**:

   o Create a TaskItem model representing a task in the database:

   csharp

```
public class TaskItem
{
    public int Id { get; set; }
    public string Title { get; set; }
    public bool IsCompleted { get; set; }
}
```

4. **Apply Migrations**:

   o Create the database schema from your models:

   bash

   dotnet ef migrations add InitialCreate
   dotnet ef database update

Performing CRUD Operations (Create, Read, Update, Delete)

1. **Create**:

   o Add new records to the database:

   csharp

```csharp
using (var context = new AppDbContext())
{
    var task = new TaskItem { Title = "Learn EF Core", IsCompleted = false };
    context.TaskItems.Add(task);
    context.SaveChanges();
}
```

2. **Read**:

   o Query records using LINQ:

   csharp

```csharp
using (var context = new AppDbContext())
```

```
{
    var tasks = context.TaskItems.ToList();
    foreach (var task in tasks)
    {
        Console.WriteLine($"{task.Id}: {task.Title} - Completed:
{task.IsCompleted}");
    }
}
```

3. **Update**:

o **Modify existing records:**

csharp

```
using (var context = new AppDbContext())
{
    var task = context.TaskItems.FirstOrDefault(t => t.Id == 1);
    if (task != null)
    {
        task.IsCompleted = true;
        context.SaveChanges();
    }
}
```

4. **Delete**:

o Remove records:

csharp

```
using (var context = new AppDbContext())
```

```
{
    var task = context.TaskItems.FirstOrDefault(t => t.Id == 1);
    if (task != null)
    {
        context.TaskItems.Remove(task);
        context.SaveChanges();
    }
}
```

Real-World Example: Building a Task Management System

Objective: Create a task management system where users can add, view, update, and delete tasks.

Step 1: Define the Model and Database Context

1. Create the TaskItem model:

    csharp

    ```
    public class TaskItem
    {
        public int Id { get; set; }
        public string Title { get; set; }
        public bool IsCompleted { get; set; }
    }
    ```

2. Create the AppDbContext:

csharp

```csharp
public class AppDbContext : DbContext
{
    public DbSet<TaskItem> TaskItems { get; set; }

    protected override void OnConfiguring(DbContextOptionsBuilder options)
    {
        options.UseSqlServer("YourConnectionString");
    }
}
```

Step 2: Create the Controller

1. Add a TaskController to handle task operations:

csharp

```csharp
using Microsoft.AspNetCore.Mvc;

public class TaskController : Controller
{
    private readonly AppDbContext _context;

    public TaskController(AppDbContext context)
    {
        _context = context;
    }
```

```csharp
public IActionResult Index()
{
    var tasks = _context.TaskItems.ToList();
    return View(tasks);
}


[HttpPost]
public IActionResult Create(string title)
{
    var task = new TaskItem { Title = title, IsCompleted = false };
    _context.TaskItems.Add(task);
    _context.SaveChanges();
    return RedirectToAction("Index");
}


public IActionResult Complete(int id)
{
    var task = _context.TaskItems.FirstOrDefault(t => t.Id == id);
    if (task != null)
    {
        task.IsCompleted = true;
        _context.SaveChanges();
    }
    return RedirectToAction("Index");
}


public IActionResult Delete(int id)
{
    var task = _context.TaskItems.FirstOrDefault(t => t.Id == id);
```

```
if (task != null)
{
    _context.TaskItems.Remove(task);
    _context.SaveChanges();
}
return RedirectToAction("Index");
    }
}
```

Step 3: Create Views

1. **Index View**:

   o File: Views/Task/Index.cshtml

   html

   @model IEnumerable<TaskItem>

   ```
   <h1>Task List</h1>
   <form method="post" asp-action="Create">
       <input type="text" name="title" placeholder="New Task" required />
       <button type="submit">Add Task</button>
   </form>

   <ul>
       @foreach (var task in Model)
       {
           <li>
   ```

```
@task.Title - Completed: @task.IsCompleted
@if (!task.IsCompleted)
{
    <a          asp-action="Complete"          asp-route-
id="@task.Id">Mark as Complete</a>
}
    <a          asp-action="Delete"          asp-route-
id="@task.Id">Delete</a>
    </li>
}
</ul>
```

Step 4: Test the Application

1. Run the application using dotnet run.
2. Navigate to /Task to manage tasks:
   o Add a new task using the form.
   o Mark tasks as complete or delete them using the provided links.

In this chapter, you learned how to work with databases in ASP.NET Core using Entity Framework Core. You set up a database, performed CRUD operations, and built a task management system. These foundational skills are essential for creating dynamic, data-driven web applications. In the next chapter, we'll explore authentication and authorization to secure your web application.

Chapter 10: Authentication and Authorization

Authentication and authorization are critical components of web application security. Authentication verifies a user's identity, while authorization determines what the authenticated user can access. This chapter introduces **ASP.NET Core Identity**, demonstrates how to implement user authentication and role-based authorization, and guides you through securing an admin panel in a real-world example.

Introduction to ASP.NET Core Identity

1. **What Is ASP.NET Core Identity?**
   - A robust framework for managing user authentication and authorization.
   - Includes built-in support for:
     - User registration and login.
     - Role-based access control.
     - Password hashing and security.
     - Email confirmation and password recovery.

2. **Key Features**:
   - Easily integrates with EF Core for storing user data in a database.

- o Extensible for custom requirements like additional user fields or external logins (Google, Facebook, etc.).

3. **Installing ASP.NET Core Identity**:
   - o Add the required packages to your project:

bash

```
dotnet                add                package
Microsoft.AspNetCore.Identity.EntityFrameworkCore
dotnet add package Microsoft.EntityFrameworkCore.SqlServer
```

4. **Setting Up ASP.NET Core Identity**:
   - o Update your AppDbContext to inherit from IdentityDbContext:

csharp

```
using Microsoft.AspNetCore.Identity.EntityFrameworkCore;
using Microsoft.EntityFrameworkCore;

public class AppDbContext : IdentityDbContext
{
    public AppDbContext(DbContextOptions<AppDbContext> options) : base(options) { }
}
```

   - o Register Identity services in Program.cs:

csharp

```
builder.Services.AddDbContext<AppDbContext>(options =>

options.UseSqlServer(builder.Configuration.GetConnectionStr
ing("DefaultConnection")));

builder.Services.AddIdentity<IdentityUser, IdentityRole>()
    .AddEntityFrameworkStores<AppDbContext>()
    .AddDefaultTokenProviders();

builder.Services.ConfigureApplicationCookie(options =>
{
    options.LoginPath = "/Account/Login";
    options.AccessDeniedPath = "/Account/AccessDenied";
});
```

o **Apply migrations:**

bash

```
dotnet ef migrations add AddIdentity
dotnet ef database update
```

Implementing User Authentication and Login Systems

1. **Setting Up Registration**:

   o Create a Register action in the AccountController:

csharp

```csharp
using Microsoft.AspNetCore.Identity;
using Microsoft.AspNetCore.Mvc;

public class AccountController : Controller
{
    private readonly UserManager<IdentityUser> _userManager;

    public AccountController(UserManager<IdentityUser> userManager)
    {
        _userManager = userManager;
    }

    [HttpGet]
    public IActionResult Register() => View();

    [HttpPost]
    public async Task<IActionResult> Register(string email, string password)
    {
        var user = new IdentityUser { UserName = email, Email = email };
        var result = await _userManager.CreateAsync(user, password);

        if (result.Succeeded)
        {
```

```
            return RedirectToAction("Login");
        }

        foreach (var error in result.Errors)
        {
            ModelState.AddModelError("", error.Description);
        }

        return View();
    }
}
```

o Create the Register.cshtml view:

html

```
<h1>Register</h1>
<form method="post">
  <div>
    <label>Email:</label>
    <input type="email" name="email" required />
  </div>
  <div>
    <label>Password:</label>
    <input type="password" name="password" required />
  </div>
  <button type="submit">Register</button>
</form>
```

2. Setting Up Login:

○ Add a Login action in AccountController:

csharp

```
private readonly SignInManager<IdentityUser> _signInManager;

public AccountController(SignInManager<IdentityUser> signInManager)
{
    _signInManager = signInManager;
}

[HttpGet]
public IActionResult Login() => View();

[HttpPost]
public async Task<IActionResult> Login(string email, string password)
{
    var result = await _signInManager.PasswordSignInAsync(email, password, false, false);

    if (result.Succeeded)
    {
        return RedirectToAction("Index", "Home");
    }

    ModelState.AddModelError("", "Invalid login attempt.");
```

```
    return View();
}
```

o   Create the Login.cshtml view:

html

```
<h1>Login</h1>
<form method="post">
  <div>
    <label>Email:</label>
    <input type="email" name="email" required />
  </div>
  <div>
    <label>Password:</label>
    <input type="password" name="password" required />
  </div>
  <button type="submit">Login</button>
</form>
```

Role-Based Authorization

1. **Defining Roles**:
   o   Add roles during application initialization:

   csharp

   ```
   public static async Task SeedRoles(IServiceProvider
   serviceProvider)
   ```

```
{
    var              roleManager              =
serviceProvider.GetRequiredService<RoleManager<IdentityR
ole>>();

    if (!await roleManager.RoleExistsAsync("Admin"))
    {
        await              roleManager.CreateAsync(new
IdentityRole("Admin"));
    }
}
```

2. **Assigning Roles to Users**:

- o Assign a role to a user:

csharp

```
var              user              =              await
_userManager.FindByEmailAsync("admin@example.com");
await _userManager.AddToRoleAsync(user, "Admin");
```

3. **Authorizing Access**:

- o Use the [Authorize] attribute to restrict access:

csharp

```
[Authorize(Roles = "Admin")]
public IActionResult AdminPanel()
{
    return View();
```

}

Real-World Example: Securing an Admin Panel

Objective: Create a secure admin panel accessible only to users with the "Admin" role.

Step 1: Create the Admin Panel Controller and View

1. Add an AdminController:

csharp

```csharp
using Microsoft.AspNetCore.Authorization;

[Authorize(Roles = "Admin")]
public class AdminController : Controller
{
    public IActionResult Index()
    {
        return View();
    }
}
```

2. Create the Index.cshtml view:

html

```html
<h1>Admin Panel</h1>
```

```
<p>Welcome, Admin!</p>
```

Step 2: Restrict Access

1. Ensure only authenticated users can access the admin panel:

csharp

```csharp
builder.Services.AddControllersWithViews(options =>
{
    options.Filters.Add(new AuthorizeFilter());
});
```

Step 3: Test the Application

1. Run the application using dotnet run.
2. Register a user and assign them the "Admin" role.
3. Log in as the admin user and navigate to /Admin.

In this chapter, you learned how to implement authentication and authorization using ASP.NET Core Identity. You built a secure login and registration system, configured role-based access control, and created a secure admin panel as a real-world example. These concepts form the foundation of securing modern web applications. In the next chapter, we'll explore handling APIs in ASP.NET Core.

Chapter 11: Handling APIs in ASP.NET Core

APIs (Application Programming Interfaces) play a crucial role in modern web applications by enabling communication between systems. In this chapter, we'll explore RESTful APIs, how to create them in ASP.NET Core, consume third-party APIs, and integrate a real-world example of a weather API into a website.

Understanding RESTful APIs

1. **What Are RESTful APIs?**
   - REST (Representational State Transfer) is an architectural style for designing networked applications.
   - RESTful APIs adhere to REST principles, providing a standard way for systems to interact.

2. **Key Characteristics of RESTful APIs**:
   - **Stateless**: Each request contains all the information needed for the server to process it.
   - **Uniform Interface**: Standardized endpoints (GET, POST, PUT, DELETE) and formats (e.g., JSON).
   - **Resource-Based**: Resources (e.g., users, products) are identified by URIs.

3. **Common HTTP Methods**:

Method	Purpose	Example
GET	Retrieve data	/api/products
POST	Create a new resource	/api/products
PUT	Update an existing resource	/api/products/1
DELETE	Remove a resource	/api/products/1

4. **Advantages of RESTful APIs**:
   o Scalability and flexibility.
   o Easy integration with client-side applications and third-party systems.

Creating APIs with ASP.NET Core

1. **Set Up the Project**:
   o Create a new API project:

   bash

   ```
   dotnet new webapi -n MyFirstAPI
   cd MyFirstAPI
   ```

2. **Define the Model**:

- o Example: Create a Product model.

  csharp

```csharp
public class Product
{
    public int Id { get; set; }
    public string Name { get; set; }
    public decimal Price { get; set; }
}
```

3. **Create a Controller**:

- o Add a ProductsController to handle API requests.

  csharp

```csharp
using Microsoft.AspNetCore.Mvc;

[ApiController]
[Route("api/[controller]")]
public class ProductsController : ControllerBase
{
    private static List<Product> Products = new List<Product>
    {
        new Product { Id = 1, Name = "Laptop", Price = 999.99M
    },
        new Product { Id = 2, Name = "Smartphone", Price =
499.99M }
    };
```

```csharp
[HttpGet]
public IActionResult GetAll()
{
    return Ok(Products);
}

[HttpGet("{id}")]
public IActionResult GetById(int id)
{
    var product = Products.FirstOrDefault(p => p.Id == id);
    if (product == null) return NotFound();
    return Ok(product);
}

[HttpPost]
public IActionResult Create(Product product)
{
    product.Id = Products.Max(p => p.Id) + 1;
    Products.Add(product);
    return CreatedAtAction(nameof(GetById), new { id =
product.Id }, product);
}

[HttpPut("{id}")]
public IActionResult Update(int id, Product updatedProduct)
{
    var product = Products.FirstOrDefault(p => p.Id == id);
    if (product == null) return NotFound();
    product.Name = updatedProduct.Name;
```

```
        product.Price = updatedProduct.Price;

        return NoContent();

    }


    [HttpDelete("{id}")]

    public IActionResult Delete(int id)

    {

        var product = Products.FirstOrDefault(p => p.Id == id);

        if (product == null) return NotFound();

        Products.Remove(product);

        return NoContent();

    }

}
```

4. **Run the Application**:

   o   Start the application:

   bash

   dotnet run

   o   Test endpoints using tools like **Postman** or **curl**.

Consuming Third-Party APIs in Your Application

1. **Why Consume APIs?**

o To integrate data or services from external systems, such as weather, payment gateways, or mapping services.

2. **Using HttpClient in ASP.NET Core**:

o Example: Fetching data from a public API.

csharp

```
using System.Net.Http;
using System.Text.Json;

public class WeatherService
{
    private readonly HttpClient _httpClient;

    public WeatherService(HttpClient httpClient)
    {
        _httpClient = httpClient;
    }

    public async Task<string> GetWeatherAsync(string city)
    {
        var response = await _httpClient.GetAsync($"https://api.openweathermap.org/data/2.5/weather?q={city}&appid=YourAPIKey");
        response.EnsureSuccessStatusCode();

        var content = await response.Content.ReadAsStringAsync();
```

```
        var                weatherData          =
JsonSerializer.Deserialize<dynamic>(content);
        return weatherData["weather"][0]["description"];
    }
}
```

3. **Register HttpClient in Dependency Injection**:

   o Configure HttpClient in Program.cs:

   csharp

   ```csharp
   builder.Services.AddHttpClient<WeatherService>();
   ```

Real-World Example: Integrating a Weather API into a Website

Objective: Build a feature that displays current weather information for a city using the OpenWeather API.

Step 1: Create the Weather Service

- Define the WeatherService class:

csharp

```csharp
public class WeatherService
{
    private readonly HttpClient _httpClient;
```

```csharp
    public WeatherService(HttpClient httpClient)
    {
      _httpClient = httpClient;
    }

    public async Task<string> GetWeatherAsync(string city)
    {
      var response = await _httpClient.GetAsync($"https://api.openweathermap.org/data/2.5/weather?q={city}&appid=YourAPIKey");
      response.EnsureSuccessStatusCode();

      var content = await response.Content.ReadAsStringAsync();
      var weatherData = JsonSerializer.Deserialize<dynamic>(content);
      return weatherData["weather"][0]["description"];
    }
}
```

Step 2: Create the Controller

- Add a WeatherController:

csharp

```csharp
public class WeatherController : Controller
{
    private readonly WeatherService _weatherService;

    public WeatherController(WeatherService weatherService)
```

```
    {
        _weatherService = weatherService;
    }


    [HttpGet]
    public IActionResult Index() => View();


    [HttpPost]
    public async Task<IActionResult> Index(string city)
    {
        var weather = await _weatherService.GetWeatherAsync(city);
        ViewData["Weather"] = weather;
        return View();
    }
}
```

Step 3: Create the Razor View

- Create Index.cshtml in Views/Weather:

html

```html
<h1>Weather Checker</h1>
<form method="post">
    <label for="city">Enter City:</label>
    <input id="city" name="city" required />
    <button type="submit">Get Weather</button>
</form>
```

```
@if (ViewData["Weather"] != null)
{
    <p>Current Weather: @ViewData["Weather"]</p>
}
```

Step 4: Test the Application

1. Run the application using dotnet run.
2. Navigate to /Weather in your browser.
3. Enter a city name to retrieve and display its weather description.

In this chapter, you explored RESTful APIs, learned how to create APIs in ASP.NET Core, and integrated third-party APIs into your application. The real-world example of integrating a weather API demonstrated how to use HttpClient and display dynamic data on a website. In the next chapter, we'll dive into advanced routing and middleware concepts in ASP.NET Core.

Chapter 12: Advanced Routing and Middleware

Middleware and routing are at the core of ASP.NET Core's request-handling pipeline. Middleware processes requests and responses, while routing maps incoming requests to specific endpoints. In this chapter, you'll learn about middleware, advanced routing techniques, and how to create custom middleware for localization.

Using Middleware for Request Handling

1. **What Is Middleware?**
   - o Middleware is software that intercepts and processes HTTP requests and responses.
   - o In ASP.NET Core, middleware components are executed in a pipeline to handle requests.
2. **Built-In Middleware**:
   - o Commonly used middleware components include:
     - ▪ **Static Files Middleware**: Serves static files like HTML, CSS, and JavaScript.
     - ▪ **Authentication Middleware**: Handles user authentication.
     - ▪ **Error Handling Middleware**: Captures and logs errors.

3. **Middleware Order**:

   o Middleware order in the pipeline affects request processing.

   o Example pipeline in Program.cs:

   csharp

   ```
   app.UseRouting();
   app.UseAuthentication();
   app.UseAuthorization();
   app.UseEndpoints(endpoints =>
   {
       endpoints.MapControllers();
   });
   ```

Building Custom Middleware Components

1. **Creating Custom Middleware**:

   o Custom middleware allows you to add custom logic to the request/response pipeline.

   o Example: Logging request details.

   csharp

   ```
   public class LoggingMiddleware
   {
       private readonly RequestDelegate _next;
   ```

```csharp
    public LoggingMiddleware(RequestDelegate next)
    {
      _next = next;
    }

    public async Task InvokeAsync(HttpContext context)
    {
      Console.WriteLine($"Request                Path:
{context.Request.Path}");
      await _next(context); // Call the next middleware in the
pipeline
    }
}
```

2. **Registering Custom Middleware**:

   o Register middleware in Program.cs:

   csharp

   ```csharp
   app.UseMiddleware<LoggingMiddleware>();
   ```

3. **Shorter Syntax**:

   o Use extension methods for simpler middleware registration:

   csharp

   ```csharp
   public static class MiddlewareExtensions
   {
   ```

```
public     static     IApplicationBuilder     UseLogging(this
IApplicationBuilder builder)
   {
       return builder.UseMiddleware<LoggingMiddleware>();
   }
}
```

```
// In Program.cs
app.UseLogging();
```

Advanced Routing Techniques

1. **Attribute-Based Routing**:
   o Use attributes to define routes directly on controller actions.

   csharp

   ```csharp
   [Route("products/{id:int}")]
   public IActionResult GetProduct(int id)
   {
       return Content($"Product ID: {id}");
   }
   ```

2. **Route Constraints**:
   o Enforce specific patterns or conditions on route parameters.

   csharp

```csharp
[Route("orders/{id:guid}")]
public IActionResult GetOrder(Guid id)
{
    return Content($"Order ID: {id}");
}
```

3. **Common Route Constraints**:

    Constraint Example   Description

    int   /products/123 Matches integers only.

    guid   /orders/{guid} Matches GUIDs.

    alpha   /tags/{alpha}   Matches alphabetic strings.

4. **Custom Route Constraints**:
    o   Create a custom constraint by implementing IRouteConstraint:

        csharp

```csharp
public class EvenNumberConstraint : IRouteConstraint
{
    public bool Match(HttpContext httpContext, IRouter route, string routeKey,
        RouteValueDictionary values, RouteDirection routeDirection)
```

```csharp
    {
        if    (values[routeKey]   is    string    value    &&
int.TryParse(value, out var number))
        {
            return number % 2 == 0;
        }
        return false;
    }
}

// Register the custom constraint
endpoints.MapControllerRoute(
    name: "EvenRoute",
    pattern: "even/{id:even}",
    defaults: new { controller = "Home", action = "Index" });
```

5. **Endpoint Routing**:

   o Simplifies routing configuration in Program.cs:

   csharp

```csharp
app.UseEndpoints(endpoints =>
{
    endpoints.MapGet("/", async context =>
    {
        await context.Response.WriteAsync("Welcome to the homepage!");
    });
});
```

Real-World Example: Creating a Localization Middleware

Objective: Create middleware to detect and apply a user's preferred language based on their request.

Step 1: Create the Middleware

1. Define LocalizationMiddleware:

csharp

```
public class LocalizationMiddleware
{
    private readonly RequestDelegate _next;

    public LocalizationMiddleware(RequestDelegate next)
    {
        _next = next;
    }

    public async Task InvokeAsync(HttpContext context)
    {
        var language = context.Request.Headers["Accept-Language"].ToString().Split(',').FirstOrDefault();
        if (!string.IsNullOrEmpty(language))
        {
            context.Items["PreferredLanguage"] = language;
        }
        else
```

```
    {
        context.Items["PreferredLanguage"] = "en-US";
    }

    await _next(context);
    }
}
```

Step 2: Register the Middleware

1. Add the middleware to the pipeline:

csharp

```
app.UseMiddleware<LocalizationMiddleware>();
```

Step 3: Use the Localization Data in Controllers

1. Retrieve the user's language preference in a controller:

csharp

```
public class HomeController : Controller
{
    public IActionResult Index()
    {
        var language = HttpContext.Items["PreferredLanguage"]?.ToString() ?? "en-US";
        return Content($"Preferred Language: {language}");
```

```
    }
  }
```

Step 4: Test the Middleware

1. Run the application using dotnet run.
2. Send a request with the Accept-Language header:
    o Example: Accept-Language: fr-FR
3. Verify the response:
    o Output: Preferred Language: fr-FR

In this chapter, you explored middleware and routing in ASP.NET Core. You learned to create custom middleware components, implement advanced routing techniques, and build a localization middleware as a real-world example. These concepts enable you to customize request handling and enhance user experiences. In the next chapter, we'll dive into high availability and disaster recovery strategies in ASP.NET Core.

Chapter 13: Session and State Management

State management is essential in web applications for maintaining user data across multiple requests. In this chapter, you'll learn how to manage user sessions, use cookies for state management, explore distributed caching, and build a real-world shopping cart system.

Managing User Sessions in ASP.NET Core

1. **What Are Sessions?**
   - A session allows storing user-specific data across multiple requests during a user's interaction with a web application.
   - Common use cases include:
     - User authentication.
     - Temporary storage of user preferences.

2. **Enabling Sessions in ASP.NET Core**:
   - Add session services in Program.cs:

     csharp

     ```
     builder.Services.AddSession();
     ```

   - Configure session middleware:

csharp

```
app.UseSession();
```

3. **Storing and Retrieving Data in Session**:

   o Example: Storing and retrieving a username.

   csharp

```
// Storing data
HttpContext.Session.SetString("UserName", "JohnDoe");

// Retrieving data
var userName = HttpContext.Session.GetString("UserName");
```

4. **Session Configuration**:

   o Customize session options:

   csharp

```
builder.Services.AddSession(options =>
{
    options.IdleTimeout = TimeSpan.FromMinutes(30);
    options.Cookie.HttpOnly = true;
    options.Cookie.IsEssential = true;
});
```

Using Cookies for State Management

1. **What Are Cookies?**

   o Cookies are small text files stored on the client's browser.

   o They enable client-side state management and are commonly used for:

     ▪ Storing user preferences.

     ▪ Tracking user activity.

2. **Creating and Reading Cookies**:

   o Example: Creating and retrieving cookies.

   csharp

   ```
   // Creating a cookie
   HttpContext.Response.Cookies.Append("Theme", "Dark");

   // Reading a cookie
   var theme = HttpContext.Request.Cookies["Theme"];
   ```

3. **Configuring Cookies**:

   o Set cookie options for security and expiration:

   csharp

   ```
   HttpContext.Response.Cookies.Append("Theme",      "Dark",
   new CookieOptions
   {
       Expires = DateTimeOffset.UtcNow.AddDays(7),
       HttpOnly = true,
       Secure = true
   ```

```
});
```

4. **Session vs. Cookies**:

   o **Session**:

   - Server-side storage.

   - Limited lifespan based on session timeout.

   o **Cookies**:

   - Client-side storage.

   - Persistent across sessions (depending on expiration).

Introduction to Distributed Caching

1. **What Is Distributed Caching?**

   o A distributed cache stores data across multiple servers, providing faster access to data and improving application scalability.

2. **Common Distributed Caching Solutions**:

   o **Redis**: An in-memory data structure store.

   o **SQL Server**: Caching with a SQL database.

3. **Setting Up Redis for ASP.NET Core**:

   o Add the Redis package:

   bash

```
dotnet                      add                      package
Microsoft.Extensions.Caching.StackExchangeRedis
```

o Configure Redis caching in Program.cs:

csharp

```csharp
builder.Services.AddStackExchangeRedisCache(options =>
{
    options.Configuration = "localhost:6379";
});
```

4. Using Distributed Caching:

o Example: Storing and retrieving cache data.

csharp

```csharp
public class CacheService
{
    private readonly IDistributedCache _cache;

    public CacheService(IDistributedCache cache)
    {
        _cache = cache;
    }

    public async Task SetCacheAsync(string key, string value)
    {
        await _cache.SetStringAsync(key, value, new
DistributedCacheEntryOptions
```

```csharp
        {
            AbsoluteExpirationRelativeToNow            =
    TimeSpan.FromMinutes(10)
            });
        }


        public async Task<string> GetCacheAsync(string key)
        {
            return await _cache.GetStringAsync(key);
        }
    }
```

Real-World Example: Building a Shopping Cart System

Objective: Create a shopping cart system where users can add, view, and remove items from their cart using sessions.

Step 1: Define the Model

- Create a CartItem model:

csharp

```csharp
public class CartItem
{
    public int Id { get; set; }
    public string Name { get; set; }
    public decimal Price { get; set; }
```

```csharp
public int Quantity { get; set; }
}
```

Step 2: Create the Controller

- Add a CartController to manage cart actions:

csharp

```csharp
using Microsoft.AspNetCore.Mvc;
using System.Text.Json;

public class CartController : Controller
{
    private const string CartSessionKey = "Cart";

    public IActionResult Index()
    {
        var cart = GetCart();
        return View(cart);
    }

    public IActionResult AddToCart(int id, string name, decimal price)
    {
        var cart = GetCart();
        var existingItem = cart.FirstOrDefault(item => item.Id == id);

        if (existingItem != null)
        {
```

```
        existingItem.Quantity++;
    }
    else
    {
        cart.Add(new CartItem { Id = id, Name = name, Price = price,
Quantity = 1 });
    }

    SaveCart(cart);
    return RedirectToAction("Index");
}

public IActionResult RemoveFromCart(int id)
{
    var cart = GetCart();
    var item = cart.FirstOrDefault(i => i.Id == id);

    if (item != null)
    {
        cart.Remove(item);
    }

    SaveCart(cart);
    return RedirectToAction("Index");
}

private List<CartItem> GetCart()
{
    var cartJson = HttpContext.Session.GetString(CartSessionKey);
```

```
        return  string.IsNullOrEmpty(cartJson) ?  new  List<CartItem>()  :
JsonSerializer.Deserialize<List<CartItem>>(cartJson);
    }

    private void SaveCart(List<CartItem> cart)
    {
        var cartJson = JsonSerializer.Serialize(cart);
        HttpContext.Session.SetString(CartSessionKey, cartJson);
    }
}
```

Step 3: Create the Views

1. Index View:

- o **File:** Views/Cart/Index.cshtml

    html

```
@model List<CartItem>

<h1>Shopping Cart</h1>
<table>
  <thead>
    <tr>
      <th>Item</th>
      <th>Price</th>
      <th>Quantity</th>
      <th>Total</th>
      <th>Action</th>
```

```
        </tr>
      </thead>
      <tbody>
        @foreach (var item in Model)
        {
          <tr>
            <td>@item.Name</td>
            <td>@item.Price.ToString("C")</td>
            <td>@item.Quantity</td>
            <td>@(item.Price                              *
item.Quantity).ToString("C")</td>
            <td>
              <a    asp-action="RemoveFromCart"    asp-route-
id="@item.Id">Remove</a>
            </td>
          </tr>
        }
      </tbody>
    </table>
```

Step 4: Test the Application

1. Run the application using dotnet run.
2. Navigate to /Cart.
3. Add items to the cart using a URL like /Cart/AddToCart?id=1&name=Product1&price=19.99.
4. View and manage the cart items.

In this chapter, you explored session and state management in ASP.NET Core, including managing user sessions, using cookies, and leveraging distributed caching. You also built a practical shopping cart system to demonstrate these concepts. In the next chapter, we'll explore asynchronous programming in ASP.NET Core.

Chapter 14: Asynchronous Programming in C#

Asynchronous programming is essential for building scalable and responsive web applications. It allows non-blocking operations, enabling servers to handle more requests simultaneously and improving user experience. This chapter explores the importance of asynchronous programming, the async and await keywords in C#, and a real-world example of building an email notification system.

Why Asynchronous Programming Is Important in Web Development

1. **Concurrency and Scalability**:
   o Asynchronous programming allows a single server to handle multiple requests without waiting for each one to complete.
   o Ideal for operations that involve I/O-bound tasks, such as database queries or API calls.

2. **Non-Blocking Operations**:
   o Prevents the application from freezing or becoming unresponsive while waiting for a long-running task.

3. **Improved User Experience**:

- o Users experience faster responses as the application remains responsive even during heavy processing.

4. **Common Use Cases**:
    - o Fetching data from external APIs.
    - o Sending emails or processing background jobs.
    - o Reading and writing files.

Using async and await in C#

1. **Understanding async and await**:
    - o The async modifier marks a method as asynchronous.
    - o The await keyword pauses the execution of the method until the awaited task is complete.

Example:

csharp

```csharp
public async Task<string> FetchDataAsync()
{
    await Task.Delay(2000); // Simulates a delay
    return "Data fetched";
}
```

2. **Creating Asynchronous Methods**:
    - o A method with async must return one of the following types:

- Task: For methods that do not return a value.
- Task<T>: For methods that return a value.
- void: For event handlers.

Example:

csharp

```csharp
public async Task ProcessDataAsync()
{
    Console.WriteLine("Processing started...");
    await Task.Delay(3000); // Simulate a 3-second delay
    Console.WriteLine("Processing completed!");
}
```

3. **Error Handling in Async Methods**:
   o Use try-catch blocks to handle exceptions in asynchronous methods.
   o Example:

   csharp

   ```csharp
   public async Task FetchDataWithErrorHandlingAsync()
   {
       try
       {
           var data = await GetDataAsync();
           Console.WriteLine(data);
       }
       catch (Exception ex)
   ```

```
    {
        Console.WriteLine($"An error occurred: {ex.Message}");
    }
}
```

4. **Combining Multiple Asynchronous Tasks**:

   o Use Task.WhenAll to run multiple asynchronous tasks in parallel.

   csharp

```
public async Task ProcessMultipleTasksAsync()
{
    var task1 = Task.Delay(2000);
    var task2 = Task.Delay(3000);

    await Task.WhenAll(task1, task2);
    Console.WriteLine("All tasks completed!");
}
```

Real-World Example: Building an Email Notification System
Objective: Create an email notification system that sends emails asynchronously to multiple recipients.

Step 1: Set Up the Email Service

1. **Install Required NuGet Package**:

o   Use the System.Net.Mail or a library like **MailKit** for sending emails.

bash

dotnet add package MailKit

2. **Create the Email Service**:

csharp

```
using MailKit.Net.Smtp;
using MimeKit;
using System.Threading.Tasks;

public class EmailService
{
   public async Task SendEmailAsync(string recipientEmail, string subject, string messageBody)
   {
      var emailMessage = new MimeMessage();
      emailMessage.From.Add(new   MailboxAddress("Your   App", "yourapp@example.com"));
      emailMessage.To.Add(new MailboxAddress("", recipientEmail));
      emailMessage.Subject = subject;

      emailMessage.Body = new TextPart("plain")
      {
         Text = messageBody
      };
```

```
using (var client = new SmtpClient())
{
    await client.ConnectAsync("smtp.example.com", 587, false);
    await        client.AuthenticateAsync("yourapp@example.com",
"yourpassword");
    await client.SendAsync(emailMessage);
    await client.DisconnectAsync(true);
}
}
}
```

Step 2: Create the Controller

1. **Add the EmailController:**

csharp

```
using Microsoft.AspNetCore.Mvc;

public class EmailController : Controller
{
    private readonly EmailService _emailService;

    public EmailController(EmailService emailService)
    {
        _emailService = emailService;
    }
```

```
public IActionResult Index() => View();

[HttpPost]
public async Task<IActionResult> SendEmails(List<string> recipients)
{
    var tasks = recipients.Select(email =>
        _emailService.SendEmailAsync(email, "Notification", "This is a test email."));

    await Task.WhenAll(tasks);

    ViewData["Message"] = "Emails sent successfully!";
    return View("Index");
}
}
```

Step 3: Create the Razor View

1. **Index View**:
   o **File**: Views/Email/Index.cshtml

   html

   ```
   <h1>Email Notification System</h1>
   <form method="post">
       <label for="recipients">Recipients (comma-separated):</label>
   ```

```html
<textarea id="recipients" name="recipients" rows="4"
cols="50"></textarea>
    <button type="submit">Send Emails</button>
</form>

@if (ViewData["Message"] != null)
{
    <p>@ViewData["Message"]</p>
}
```

Step 4: Test the Application

1. Run the application using dotnet run.

2. Navigate to /Email.

3. Enter recipient email addresses and send test emails.

In this chapter, you learned the importance of asynchronous programming in web development, explored async and await in C#, and built a real-world email notification system. Asynchronous programming is a vital skill for creating efficient and scalable web applications. In the next chapter, we'll dive into building and consuming APIs.

Chapter 15: Dependency Injection in ASP.NET Core

Dependency Injection (DI) is a design pattern used to achieve Inversion of Control (IoC) by allowing dependencies to be provided rather than created within classes. ASP.NET Core has built-in support for DI, making it an integral part of application development. In this chapter, you'll learn the importance of DI, how to set it up in ASP.NET Core, and implement a real-world example of managing logging with DI.

Understanding Dependency Injection (DI) and Its Importance

1. **What Is Dependency Injection?**
   o Dependency Injection is a technique where objects are provided with their dependencies by an external source (often a DI container) rather than creating them internally.
   o It promotes loose coupling and better testability.

2. **Key Concepts of DI**:
   o **Service**: A reusable component or object that performs a task.
   o **Client**: A class that depends on a service.

- o **Injector**: The mechanism that provides the service to the client.

Example Without DI:

csharp

```
public class UserService
{
    private readonly Logger _logger = new Logger();

    public void PerformAction()
    {
        _logger.Log("Action performed.");
    }
}
```

Example With DI:

csharp

```
public class UserService
{
    private readonly ILogger _logger;

    public UserService(ILogger logger)
    {
        _logger = logger;
    }

    public void PerformAction()
```

```
    {
        _logger.Log("Action performed.");
    }
}
```

3. **Advantages of DI**:
   - o **Loose Coupling**: Classes don't manage their dependencies, making them easier to modify.
   - o **Testability**: Dependencies can be mocked for unit testing.
   - o **Scalability**: Services can be reused and configured globally.

Setting Up and Using DI in ASP.NET Core

1. **DI in ASP.NET Core**:
   - o ASP.NET Core provides a built-in IoC container for managing dependencies.
   - o Services are registered in the container and injected where needed.

2. **Service Lifetimes**:
   - o **Transient**:
     - ▪ A new instance is created every time the service is requested.
     - ▪ Use for lightweight and stateless services.

csharp

```
builder.Services.AddTransient<IMyService, MyService>();
```

- o **Scoped**:
  - A single instance is created per request.
  - Use for request-specific operations, like database contexts.

csharp

```
builder.Services.AddScoped<IMyService, MyService>();
```

- o **Singleton**:
  - A single instance is created for the entire application lifetime.
  - Use for shared state services or caches.

csharp

```
builder.Services.AddSingleton<IMyService, MyService>();
```

3. **Registering Services**:
   - o Register services in Program.cs:

csharp

```
builder.Services.AddTransient<IMyService, MyService>();
```

4. **Injecting Services**:

    o Inject the registered service into a controller or other class:

csharp

```csharp
public class HomeController : Controller
{
    private readonly IMyService _myService;

    public HomeController(IMyService myService)
    {
        _myService = myService;
    }

    public IActionResult Index()
    {
        _myService.PerformTask();
        return View();
    }
}
```

Real-World Example: Managing Logging with DI

Objective: Use DI to manage logging services in an ASP.NET Core application.

Step 1: Create the Logging Service

1. Define the ILogger interface:

csharp

```csharp
public interface ILogger
{
    void Log(string message);
}
```

2. Implement the ConsoleLogger class:

csharp

```csharp
public class ConsoleLogger : ILogger
{
    public void Log(string message)
    {
        Console.WriteLine($"[LOG]: {message}");
    }
}
```

Step 2: Register the Service

1. Add the logging service in Program.cs:

csharp

```csharp
builder.Services.AddSingleton<ILogger, ConsoleLogger>();
```

Step 3: Use the Service in a Controller

1. Inject and use the logger in the HomeController:

csharp

```
public class HomeController : Controller
{
  private readonly ILogger _logger;

  public HomeController(ILogger logger)
  {
    _logger = logger;
  }

  public IActionResult Index()
  {
    _logger.Log("Visited Home Page");
    return View();
  }
}
```

Step 4: Test the Application

1. Run the application using dotnet run.

2. Navigate to the homepage.

3. Verify that the log message is displayed in the console:

markdown

[LOG]: Visited Home Page

Expanding the Example

1. **Adding a File Logger**:
   - Implement a logger that writes to a file:

   csharp

   ```csharp
   public class FileLogger : ILogger
   {
       private readonly string _filePath = "log.txt";

       public void Log(string message)
       {
           File.AppendAllText(_filePath,                    $"[LOG]:
   {message}{Environment.NewLine}");
       }
   }
   ```

2. **Switching Loggers**:
   - Update the registration in Program.cs to use FileLogger instead of ConsoleLogger:

   csharp

   ```csharp
   builder.Services.AddSingleton<ILogger, FileLogger>();
   ```

3. **Testing the File Logger**:

    ○ Run the application and verify that logs are written to log.txt.

In this chapter, you learned the fundamentals of dependency injection, how it's implemented in ASP.NET Core, and the importance of service lifetimes. You also built a real-world logging system using DI, demonstrating its flexibility and reusability. In the next chapter, we'll explore advanced configuration and options in ASP.NET Core.

Chapter 16: Unit Testing and Debugging

Unit testing and debugging are critical practices for ensuring the reliability and correctness of software. In this chapter, you'll learn the basics of unit testing in C#, how to write tests for ASP.NET Core applications, and debugging techniques using Visual Studio. A real-world example of testing and debugging a user authentication module will solidify these concepts.

Introduction to Unit Testing in C#

1. **What Is Unit Testing?**
   - Unit testing involves testing individual components or functions of an application in isolation to ensure they work as expected.
   - Focuses on small, testable units such as methods or classes.

2. **Why Unit Testing Matters**:
   - **Early Detection**: Identifies bugs early in development.
   - **Code Quality**: Ensures code meets functional requirements.
   - **Refactoring Safety**: Reduces risk when modifying code.

3. **Unit Testing Frameworks in C#:**

   o **xUnit**: A popular, open-source framework for testing .NET applications.

   o **NUnit**: Another widely used framework.

   o **MSTest**: Microsoft's built-in testing framework for .NET.

4. **Setting Up xUnit**:

   o Add the xUnit NuGet package:

   bash

   ```
   dotnet add package xunit
   dotnet add package xunit.runner.visualstudio
   ```

Writing Tests for ASP.NET Core Applications

1. **Setting Up a Test Project**:

   o Create a new test project:

   bash

   ```
   dotnet new xunit -n MyApp.Tests
   cd MyApp.Tests
   ```

   o Add a reference to the main application project:

   bash

```
dotnet add reference ../MyApp/MyApp.csproj
```

2. Creating a Sample Unit Test:

- Test a utility method, e.g., a Calculator class:

csharp

```csharp
public class Calculator
{
    public int Add(int a, int b) => a + b;
}
```

- Write a test for the Add method:

csharp

```csharp
using Xunit;

public class CalculatorTests
{
    [Fact]
    public void Add_ReturnsCorrectSum()
    {
        // Arrange
        var calculator = new Calculator();

        // Act
        var result = calculator.Add(2, 3);

        // Assert
```

```
        Assert.Equal(5, result);
    }
}
```

3. **Running Tests**:
   - o Run tests using the .NET CLI:

   bash

   dotnet test

   - o Use Visual Studio's Test Explorer for a graphical view of test results.

4. **Testing ASP.NET Core Controllers**:
   - o Test a controller action using a mock service:

   csharp

   ```csharp
   public class HomeController : Controller
   {
       private readonly IMyService _service;

       public HomeController(IMyService service)
       {
           _service = service;
       }

       public IActionResult Index()
       {
           var data = _service.GetData();
   ```

```
        return View(data);
    }
}
```

- o **Write a test with a mocked service:**

csharp

```
using Moq;
using Xunit;

public class HomeControllerTests
{
    [Fact]
    public void Index_ReturnsViewResultWithModel()
    {
        // Arrange
        var mockService = new Mock<IMyService>();
        mockService.Setup(s   =>   s.GetData()).Returns(new
List<string> { "Item1", "Item2" });

        var         controller        =          new
HomeController(mockService.Object);

        // Act
        var result = controller.Index();

        // Assert
        var viewResult = Assert.IsType<ViewResult>(result);
```

```
Assert.IsAssignableFrom<IEnumerable<string>>(viewResult.
Model);
    }
}
```

Debugging Techniques Using Visual Studio

1. **Breakpoints**:
   - Set breakpoints to pause code execution and inspect variables.
   - Use **Conditional Breakpoints** to pause execution only when specific conditions are met.

2. **Immediate Window**:
   - Evaluate expressions and execute commands at runtime.
   - Access via **Debug > Windows > Immediate**.

3. **Watch Window**:
   - Monitor variable values and expressions while debugging.
   - Add variables to the **Watch Window** to track their state.

4. **Call Stack**:
   - Examine the sequence of method calls leading to the current breakpoint.
   - Helps trace the origin of errors.

5. **Step Operations**:

   o **Step Into (F11)**: Enters the method being called.

   o **Step Over (F10)**: Executes the method without entering it.

   o **Step Out (Shift+F11)**: Exits the current method.

Real-World Example: Testing and Debugging a User Authentication Module

Objective: Test and debug a login system with user authentication.

Step 1: Create the Login Service

1. Define the IAuthService interface:

   csharp

   ```csharp
   public interface IAuthService
   {
       bool Login(string username, string password);
   }
   ```

2. Implement the AuthService class:

   csharp

   ```csharp
   public class AuthService : IAuthService
   ```

```
{
    public bool Login(string username, string password)
    {
        return username == "admin" && password == "password123";
    }
}
```

Step 2: Test the Authentication Service

1. Write tests for AuthService:

csharp

```csharp
using Xunit;

public class AuthServiceTests
{
    [Fact]
    public void Login_ValidCredentials_ReturnsTrue()
    {
        // Arrange
        var authService = new AuthService();

        // Act
        var result = authService.Login("admin", "password123");

        // Assert
        Assert.True(result);
    }
```

```
[Fact]
public void Login_InvalidCredentials_ReturnsFalse()
{
    // Arrange
    var authService = new AuthService();

    // Act
    var result = authService.Login("user", "wrongpassword");

    // Assert
    Assert.False(result);
}
}
```

Step 3: Debug the Login Controller

1. Create a LoginController:

csharp

```
public class LoginController : Controller
{
    private readonly IAuthService _authService;

    public LoginController(IAuthService authService)
    {
        _authService = authService;
    }
```

```
public IActionResult Login(string username, string password)
{
    if (_authService.Login(username, password))
    {
        return RedirectToAction("Index", "Home");
    }

    ViewData["Error"] = "Invalid login attempt.";
    return View();
}
}
```

2. Debugging Steps:

   o   Set a breakpoint in the Login method.

   o   Input invalid credentials and observe how the code handles them.

   o   Inspect the state of username, password, and ViewData in the **Watch Window**.

In this chapter, you learned the fundamentals of unit testing and debugging in ASP.NET Core applications. You explored how to write unit tests for services and controllers, use debugging tools in Visual Studio, and applied these skills in a real-world authentication module. These practices enhance the reliability and maintainability of your applications.

Chapter 17: Advanced Features in ASP.NET Core

ASP.NET Core offers advanced features for creating sophisticated web applications. In this chapter, you'll explore **SignalR** for real-time communication, implement **background tasks** using hosted services, and build a real-world example of a real-time chat application.

SignalR for Real-Time Web Applications

1. **What Is SignalR?**
   - SignalR is a library for adding real-time functionality to web applications.
   - Enables server-side updates to clients without requiring clients to repeatedly request updates (e.g., polling).
   - Supports WebSockets, Server-Sent Events (SSE), and Long Polling.

2. **Common Use Cases**:
   - Chat applications.
   - Live dashboards and notifications.
   - Real-time multiplayer games.

3. **Setting Up SignalR**:
   - Add SignalR to your project:

bash

```
dotnet add package Microsoft.AspNetCore.SignalR
```

- o Configure SignalR in Program.cs:

csharp

```csharp
builder.Services.AddSignalR();
app.UseEndpoints(endpoints =>
{
    endpoints.MapHub<ChatHub>("/chatHub");
});
```

4. **Creating a SignalR Hub**:

- o Define a ChatHub for handling client-server communication:

csharp

```csharp
using Microsoft.AspNetCore.SignalR;

public class ChatHub : Hub
{
    public async Task SendMessage(string user, string message)
    {
        await Clients.All.SendAsync("ReceiveMessage", user, message);
    }
}
```

5. **Connecting the Client**:

    o Include the SignalR JavaScript library:

        html

```html
<script src="https://cdnjs.cloudflare.com/ajax/libs/microsoft-signalr/5.0.13/signalr.min.js"></script>
```

    o Set up the client-side connection:

        html

```html
<script>
    const connection = new signalR.HubConnectionBuilder().withUrl("/chatHub").build();

    connection.on("ReceiveMessage", (user, message) => {
        const li = document.createElement("li");
        li.textContent = `${user}: ${message}`;

document.getElementById("messagesList").appendChild(li);
    });

    connection.start().catch(err => console.error(err.toString()));


document.getElementById("sendButton").addEventListener("click", () => {
        const user = document.getElementById("userInput").value;
```

```
        const                 message              =
document.getElementById("messageInput").value;
        connection.invoke("SendMessage",            user,
    message).catch(err => console.error(err.toString())));
    });
</script>
```

Background Tasks with Hosted Services

1. **What Are Hosted Services?**
   - Hosted services are background tasks that run alongside your ASP.NET Core application.
   - Ideal for periodic or long-running tasks like sending emails, processing queues, or cleanup operations.

2. **Types of Hosted Services**:
   - **IHostedService**: A simple interface for creating background services.
   - **BackgroundService**: A base class for implementing long-running tasks.

3. **Creating a Hosted Service**:
   - Example: A service that logs a message every minute.

   csharp

```csharp
public class LoggingService : BackgroundService
{
    private readonly ILogger<LoggingService> _logger;
```

```csharp
public LoggingService(ILogger<LoggingService> logger)
{
    _logger = logger;
}

protected override async Task
ExecuteAsync(CancellationToken stoppingToken)
{
    while (!stoppingToken.IsCancellationRequested)
    {
        _logger.LogInformation("Logging service running...");
        await Task.Delay(TimeSpan.FromMinutes(1),
stoppingToken);
    }
}
```

4. **Registering the Hosted Service**:
   o Add the hosted service in Program.cs:

   csharp

   builder.Services.AddHostedService<LoggingService>();

Real-World Example: Building a Real-Time Chat Application

Objective: Create a real-time chat application using SignalR and ASP.NET Core.

Step 1: Create the SignalR Hub

1. Define the ChatHub:

csharp

```
using Microsoft.AspNetCore.SignalR;

public class ChatHub : Hub
{
    public async Task SendMessage(string user, string message)
    {
        await Clients.All.SendAsync("ReceiveMessage", user, message);
    }
}
```

Step 2: Configure SignalR

1. Update Program.cs to configure SignalR:

csharp

```
builder.Services.AddSignalR();
app.UseEndpoints(endpoints =>
{
    endpoints.MapHub<ChatHub>("/chatHub");
});
```

Step 3: Create the Razor View

1. Create a Chat.cshtml file in Views/Chat:

html

```
@page
<h1>Real-Time Chat</h1>
<input id="userInput" type="text" placeholder="Your name" />
<input id="messageInput" type="text" placeholder="Type a message" />
<button id="sendButton">Send</button>

<ul id="messagesList"></ul>

<script src="https://cdnjs.cloudflare.com/ajax/libs/microsoft-signalr/5.0.13/signalr.min.js"></script>
<script>
    const connection = new signalR.HubConnectionBuilder().withUrl("/chatHub").build();

    connection.on("ReceiveMessage", (user, message) => {
        const li = document.createElement("li");
        li.textContent = `${user}: ${message}`;
        document.getElementById("messagesList").appendChild(li);
    });

    connection.start().catch(err => console.error(err.toString()));
```

```
document.getElementById("sendButton").addEventListener("click",
() => {
    const user = document.getElementById("userInput").value;
    const           message           =
document.getElementById("messageInput").value;
    connection.invoke("SendMessage", user, message).catch(err =>
console.error(err.toString()));
    });
</script>
```

Step 4: Run the Application

1. Start the application using dotnet run.
2. Navigate to /Chat.
3. Open multiple browser tabs and send messages to see real-time updates.

In this chapter, you explored advanced features of ASP.NET Core, including real-time communication with SignalR and background tasks with hosted services. The real-world example of a real-time chat application demonstrated the power of these tools. In the next chapter, we'll dive into deploying ASP.NET Core applications.

Chapter 18: Building and Consuming APIs

APIs (Application Programming Interfaces) are essential for modern web and mobile applications, enabling communication between back-end services and front-end or mobile apps. In this chapter, you'll learn how to create APIs in ASP.NET Core, implement GraphQL, and build a real-world API for a mobile e-commerce app.

Creating APIs for Front-End and Mobile Apps

1. **What Is an API?**
   - o An API allows applications to communicate by exposing endpoints for performing operations such as data retrieval, creation, and updates.
   - o ASP.NET Core is well-suited for building RESTful APIs that follow standard HTTP protocols.

2. **Setting Up an API Project**:
   - o Create a new Web API project:

   bash

   ```
   dotnet new webapi -n ECommerceAPI
   cd ECommerceAPI
   ```

3. **Defining Models**:

   o Example: Define a Product model for an e-commerce API:

   csharp

```csharp
public class Product
{
    public int Id { get; set; }
    public string Name { get; set; }
    public decimal Price { get; set; }
    public string Description { get; set; }
}
```

4. **Creating a Controller**:

   o Add a ProductsController with basic CRUD operations:

   csharp

```csharp
using Microsoft.AspNetCore.Mvc;

[ApiController]
[Route("api/[controller]")]
public class ProductsController : ControllerBase
{
    private static List<Product> Products = new List<Product>
    {
        new Product { Id = 1, Name = "Laptop", Price = 999.99M,
Description = "High-performance laptop" },
```

```
    new Product { Id = 2, Name = "Smartphone", Price =
699.99M, Description = "Latest model smartphone" }
    };

    [HttpGet]
    public IActionResult GetAll()
    {
        return Ok(Products);
    }

    [HttpGet("{id}")]
    public IActionResult GetById(int id)
    {
        var product = Products.FirstOrDefault(p => p.Id == id);
        if (product == null) return NotFound();
        return Ok(product);
    }

    [HttpPost]
    public IActionResult Create(Product product)
    {
        product.Id = Products.Max(p => p.Id) + 1;
        Products.Add(product);
        return CreatedAtAction(nameof(GetById), new { id =
product.Id }, product);
    }

    [HttpPut("{id}")]
    public IActionResult Update(int id, Product updatedProduct)
    {
```

```
    var product = Products.FirstOrDefault(p => p.Id == id);
    if (product == null) return NotFound();
    product.Name = updatedProduct.Name;
    product.Price = updatedProduct.Price;
    product.Description = updatedProduct.Description;
    return NoContent();
}


[HttpDelete("{id}")]
public IActionResult Delete(int id)
{
    var product = Products.FirstOrDefault(p => p.Id == id);
    if (product == null) return NotFound();
    Products.Remove(product);
    return NoContent();
}
}
```

5. **Testing the API**:

   o Run the application using:

   bash

   dotnet run

   o Test endpoints using **Postman** or **curl**:
      - GET /api/products
      - POST /api/products
      - PUT /api/products/{id}
      - DELETE /api/products/{id}

Implementing GraphQL in ASP.NET Core

1. **What Is GraphQL?**
   - o GraphQL is a query language for APIs that allows clients to request only the data they need, improving efficiency and flexibility.

2. **Installing GraphQL.NET**:
   - o Add the required NuGet packages:

   bash

   ```
   dotnet add package GraphQL
   dotnet add package GraphQL.Server.Transports.AspNetCore
   dotnet add package GraphQL.Server.Ui.Playground
   ```

3. **Defining a GraphQL Schema**:
   - o Create a ProductType class:

   csharp

   ```csharp
   using GraphQL.Types;

   public class ProductType : ObjectGraphType<Product>
   {
       public ProductType()
       {
           Field(x => x.Id).Description("The ID of the product.");
   ```

```
Field(x => x.Name).Description("The name of the
product.");
       Field(x => x.Price).Description("The price of the
product.");
       Field(x => x.Description).Description("The description of
the product.");
   }
}
```

4. **Creating the Query**:

o **Define a** ProductQuery **class**:

csharp

```
using GraphQL.Types;

public class ProductQuery : ObjectGraphType
{
  public ProductQuery()
  {
    Field<ListGraphType<ProductType>>(
      "products",
      resolve: context => new List<Product>
      {
        new Product { Id = 1, Name = "Laptop", Price =
999.99M, Description = "High-performance laptop" },
        new Product { Id = 2, Name = "Smartphone", Price =
699.99M, Description = "Latest model smartphone" }
      }
    );
```

```
        }
    }
```

5. **Configuring GraphQL in the Application**:

   o Add the GraphQL service:

   csharp

   ```csharp
   builder.Services.AddSingleton<ProductQuery>();
   builder.Services.AddSingleton<ProductType>();
   builder.Services.AddGraphQL(options                    =>
   options.EnableMetrics = false).AddSystemTextJson();
   ```

   o Map the GraphQL endpoint:

   csharp

   ```csharp
   app.UseGraphQL<ProductQuery>("/graphql");
   app.UseGraphQLPlayground("/ui/playground");
   ```

6. **Testing GraphQL**:

   o Run the application and navigate to /ui/playground.

   o Execute a query:

   graphql

   ```graphql
   {
     products {
       id
       name
   ```

```
                price
           }
       }
```

Real-World Example: Building an API for a Mobile E-Commerce App

Objective: Build an API to manage products and orders for a mobile e-commerce application.

Step 1: Define Models

1. Create Product and Order models:

```csharp
public class Product
{
    public int Id { get; set; }
    public string Name { get; set; }
    public decimal Price { get; set; }
}

public class Order
{
    public int Id { get; set; }
    public List<Product> Products { get; set; }
    public decimal TotalAmount { get; set; }
```

}

Step 2: Create Controllers

1. Add ProductsController and OrdersController:

csharp

```csharp
[ApiController]
[Route("api/[controller]")]
public class OrdersController : ControllerBase
{
    private static List<Order> Orders = new List<Order>();

    [HttpPost]
    public IActionResult Create(Order order)
    {
        order.Id = Orders.Count + 1;
        Orders.Add(order);
        return CreatedAtAction(nameof(GetById), new { id = order.Id },
order);
    }

    [HttpGet("{id}")]
    public IActionResult GetById(int id)
    {
        var order = Orders.FirstOrDefault(o => o.Id == id);
        if (order == null) return NotFound();
        return Ok(order);
```

```
    }
  }
```

Step 3: Test the API

1. Run the application and test the endpoints for managing products and orders using Postman or Swagger.

In this chapter, you explored how to build APIs for front-end and mobile applications, implemented GraphQL in ASP.NET Core, and created a real-world API for a mobile e-commerce app. These concepts are essential for developing scalable and efficient web services. In the next chapter, we'll focus on securing APIs with authentication and authorization.

Chapter 19: Working with Third-Party Libraries

Third-party libraries allow developers to quickly integrate robust features into applications without reinventing the wheel. This chapter explores the use of libraries like **AutoMapper** for object mapping and **Serilog** for logging. You'll also learn how to use NuGet packages effectively and implement enhanced logging with Serilog in a real-world example.

Integrating Libraries Like AutoMapper and Serilog

1. **What Is AutoMapper?**
   - AutoMapper is a library that automates the mapping of objects, simplifying the transfer of data between layers in your application.
   - Common use cases:
     - Mapping data transfer objects (DTOs) to domain models.
     - Mapping view models to business objects.
2. **What Is Serilog?**
   - Serilog is a flexible logging library for .NET.
   - Features:

- Structured logging for better querying and analysis.
- Support for multiple sinks like files, databases, and cloud services.

Using NuGet Packages in Your Projects

1. **What Is NuGet?**
   o NuGet is the package manager for .NET, offering libraries and tools to enhance development.

2. **Installing NuGet Packages**:
   o Use the .NET CLI to add packages:

   bash

   ```
   dotnet add package AutoMapper
   dotnet add package Serilog
   dotnet add package Serilog.AspNetCore
   dotnet add package Serilog.Sinks.File
   ```

3. **Managing Packages**:
   o View installed packages:

   bash

   ```
   dotnet list package
   ```

o Update a package:

bash

dotnet   add   package   <PackageName>   --version
<VersionNumber>

Integrating AutoMapper

1. **Setting Up AutoMapper**:
   o Configure AutoMapper by defining mappings in a
      Profile:

csharp

```
using AutoMapper;

public class MappingProfile : Profile
{
  public MappingProfile()
  {
    CreateMap<Product, ProductDTO>();
    CreateMap<ProductDTO, Product>();
  }
}

public class Product
{
  public int Id { get; set; }
```

```
    public string Name { get; set; }
    public decimal Price { get; set; }
}

public class ProductDTO
{
    public int Id { get; set; }
    public string Name { get; set; }
}
```

2. **Registering AutoMapper**:
   o Add AutoMapper to Program.cs:

   csharp

   ```
   builder.Services.AddAutoMapper(typeof(MappingProfile));
   ```

3. **Using AutoMapper**:
   o Inject and use IMapper:

   csharp

   ```
   public class ProductController : ControllerBase
   {
       private readonly IMapper _mapper;

       public ProductController(IMapper mapper)
       {
           _mapper = mapper;
       }
   ```

```csharp
[HttpGet]
public IActionResult GetProduct()
{
    var product = new Product { Id = 1, Name = "Laptop",
Price = 999.99M };
    var productDto = _mapper.Map<ProductDTO>(product);
    return Ok(productDto);
}
}
```

Integrating Serilog

1. **Setting Up Serilog**:
   - Configure Serilog in Program.cs:

   csharp

   ```csharp
   using Serilog;

   var logger = new LoggerConfiguration()
       .WriteTo.Console()
       .WriteTo.File("logs/log.txt",                rollingInterval:
   RollingInterval.Day)
       .CreateLogger();

   builder.Host.UseSerilog(logger);
   ```

2. **Using Serilog**:

o Inject and use ILogger<T> in controllers:

csharp

```csharp
public class HomeController : ControllerBase
{
    private readonly ILogger<HomeController> _logger;

    public HomeController(ILogger<HomeController> logger)
    {
        _logger = logger;
    }

    [HttpGet]
    public IActionResult Index()
    {
        _logger.LogInformation("Home page accessed.");
        return Ok("Welcome to the home page.");
    }
}
```

3. **Structured Logging**:

   o Log with structured data:

   csharp

```csharp
_logger.LogInformation("User {UserId} accessed the home page at {AccessTime}", userId, DateTime.UtcNow);
```

Real-World Example: Enhancing Application Logging with Serilog

Objective: Use Serilog to implement structured logging in an ASP.NET Core application.

Step 1: Configure Serilog

1. Install the required packages:

   bash

   ```
   dotnet add package Serilog
   dotnet add package Serilog.AspNetCore
   dotnet add package Serilog.Sinks.File
   ```

2. Configure Serilog in Program.cs:

   csharp

   ```
   using Serilog;

   var logger = new LoggerConfiguration()
       .WriteTo.Console()
       .WriteTo.File("logs/log.txt", rollingInterval: RollingInterval.Day)
       .CreateLogger();

   builder.Host.UseSerilog(logger);
   ```

Step 2: Implement Logging

1. Update a controller to include logging:

csharp

```csharp
public class ProductController : ControllerBase
{
    private readonly ILogger<ProductController> _logger;

    public ProductController(ILogger<ProductController> logger)
    {
        _logger = logger;
    }

    [HttpGet("{id}")]
    public IActionResult GetProduct(int id)
    {
        _logger.LogInformation("Fetching product with ID: {ProductId}", id);

        var product = new Product { Id = id, Name = "Laptop", Price = 999.99M };
        if (product == null)
        {
            _logger.LogWarning("Product with ID: {ProductId} not found.", id);
            return NotFound();
        }
```

```
    _logger.LogInformation("Product with ID: {ProductId} fetched
successfully.", id);
    return Ok(product);
  }
}
```

Step 3: Test Logging

1. Run the application and make requests to the ProductController.
2. Verify logs in the console and the logs/log.txt file.

Step 4: Analyze Logs

- Open the log file and observe structured entries:

csharp

```
[Information] Fetching product with ID: 1
[Information] Product with ID: 1 fetched successfully.
```

In this chapter, you learned how to use third-party libraries like AutoMapper and Serilog in ASP.NET Core applications. You explored how to install and manage NuGet packages and implemented enhanced logging with Serilog in a real-world example.

These tools significantly improve productivity, code readability, and maintainability.

Chapter 20: Performance Optimization

Performance optimization is crucial for creating fast and responsive ASP.NET Core applications. This chapter explores best practices for optimizing performance, including caching, compression, and bundling. A real-world example of optimizing a content-heavy website ties these techniques together.

Best Practices for Optimizing ASP.NET Core Applications

1. **Use Asynchronous Code**:
   - Implement asynchronous programming with async and await to handle I/O-bound tasks efficiently.

2. **Optimize Database Queries**:
   - Avoid unnecessary queries by leveraging **lazy loading** and **eager loading** appropriately.
   - Use **indexes** in the database to speed up query execution.

3. **Minimize HTTP Requests**:
   - Combine CSS and JavaScript files.
   - Use a Content Delivery Network (CDN) for static assets.

4. **Reduce Payload Size**:
   - Compress response data using **Gzip** or **Brotli**.

- o Minify CSS and JavaScript files.

5. **Enable Response Caching**:
    - o Cache static and dynamic content to reduce server load.

6. **Use Dependency Injection Efficiently**:
    - o Register services with appropriate lifetimes (e.g., Singleton, Scoped, Transient).

7. **Monitor and Log Performance Metrics**:
    - o Use **Application Insights**, **Serilog**, or other monitoring tools.

8. **Profile and Benchmark**:
    - o Identify bottlenecks using profiling tools like **dotTrace**, **Visual Studio Profiler**, or **BenchmarkDotNet**.

Using Caching, Compression, and Bundling

Caching

1. **In-Memory Caching**:
    - o Use in-memory caching for frequently accessed data.

    csharp

    ```
    builder.Services.AddMemoryCache();
    ```

○ Store and retrieve data:

csharp

```csharp
public class ProductService
{
    private readonly IMemoryCache _cache;

    public ProductService(IMemoryCache cache)
    {
        _cache = cache;
    }

    public Product GetProduct(int id)
    {
        if (!_cache.TryGetValue(id, out Product product))
        {
            product = FetchProductFromDatabase(id); // Simulated database fetch
            _cache.Set(id, product, TimeSpan.FromMinutes(10));
        }
        return product;
    }
}
```

2. **Distributed Caching**:

○ Use Redis or SQL Server for distributed caching in multi-server environments.

csharp

```
builder.Services.AddStackExchangeRedisCache(options =>
{
    options.Configuration = "localhost:6379";
});
```

3. Response Caching:

- Enable response caching to cache HTTP responses.

csharp

```
builder.Services.AddResponseCaching();
app.UseResponseCaching();
```

- Configure caching in controllers:

csharp

```
[ResponseCache(Duration    =    60,    Location    =
ResponseCacheLocation.Client)]
public IActionResult Index()
{
    return View();
}
```

Compression

1. Enable Gzip/Brotli Compression:

- Add the compression middleware:

csharp

```
builder.Services.AddResponseCompression(options =>
{
    options.Providers.Add<GzipCompressionProvider>();
    options.EnableForHttps = true;
});
```

o Configure compression in Program.cs:

csharp

```
app.UseResponseCompression();
```

2. Gzip Configuration:

o Use Gzip for compressing large payloads:

csharp

```
builder.Services.Configure<GzipCompressionProviderOptions
>(options =>
{
    options.Level                              =
System.IO.Compression.CompressionLevel.Optimal;
});
```

Bundling and Minification

1. What Is Bundling and Minification?

- o **Bundling**: Combines multiple CSS or JavaScript files into one.
- o **Minification**: Reduces file size by removing unnecessary characters like whitespaces and comments.

2. **Using Bundling in ASP.NET Core**:
   - o Add tools like WebOptimizer or integrate with front-end build systems (e.g., Webpack).
   - o Example with WebOptimizer:

   bash

   ```
   dotnet add package WebOptimizer.AspNetCore
   ```

   - o Configure in Program.cs:

   csharp

   ```
   builder.Services.AddWebOptimizer(pipeline =>
   {
       pipeline.AddCssBundle("/css/bundle.css", "css/*.css");
       pipeline.AddJavaScriptBundle("/js/bundle.js", "js/*.js");
   });
   app.UseWebOptimizer();
   ```

Real-World Example: Optimizing a Content-Heavy Website

Objective: Optimize a content-heavy website to improve page load times and reduce server load.

Step 1: Enable Caching

1. **Add In-Memory Caching**:

   csharp

   ```csharp
   builder.Services.AddMemoryCache();
   ```

2. **Cache Expensive Queries**:

   csharp

   ```csharp
   public class ArticleService
   {
       private readonly IMemoryCache _cache;

       public ArticleService(IMemoryCache cache)
       {
           _cache = cache;
       }

       public IEnumerable<Article> GetPopularArticles()
       {
           const string cacheKey = "PopularArticles";
           if (!_cache.TryGetValue(cacheKey, out IEnumerable<Article> articles))
   ```

```
    {
        articles = FetchArticlesFromDatabase(); // Simulate database
fetch
        _cache.Set(cacheKey, articles, TimeSpan.FromMinutes(15));
    }
    return articles;
  }
}
```

Step 2: Enable Compression

1. **Add Response Compression**:

csharp

```
builder.Services.AddResponseCompression();
app.UseResponseCompression();
```

2. **Test Compression**:
   o Inspect HTTP responses using browser developer tools to verify compressed payloads.

Step 3: Bundle and Minify Assets

1. **Install WebOptimizer**:

bash

dotnet add package WebOptimizer.AspNetCore

2. **Bundle CSS and JavaScript**:

csharp

```
builder.Services.AddWebOptimizer(pipeline =>
{
    pipeline.AddCssBundle("/css/bundle.css", "wwwroot/css/*.css");
    pipeline.AddJavaScriptBundle("/js/bundle.js", "wwwroot/js/*.js");
});
app.UseWebOptimizer();
```

3. **Update Views to Use Bundled Files**:

html

```
<link href="/css/bundle.css" rel="stylesheet">
<script src="/js/bundle.js"></script>
```

Step 4: Measure Performance

1. **Use Tools**:
   o Browser developer tools for network performance.
   o **Lighthouse** for overall performance scoring.
   o **dotnet trace** for server-side profiling.
2. **Analyze Metrics**:

- o Compare page load times before and after optimization.
- o Check reduced HTTP request count and payload size.

In this chapter, you learned best practices for optimizing ASP.NET Core applications, including caching, compression, and bundling. These techniques were applied in a real-world example to optimize a content-heavy website. By implementing these strategies, you can significantly improve application performance and user experience.

Chapter 21: Deploying Your Application

Deploying an application is the final step in delivering it to users. Proper deployment ensures that the application runs efficiently, securely, and reliably in the production environment. This chapter covers preparing your ASP.NET Core application for deployment, explores deployment options like Azure, AWS, and on-premises servers, and guides you through creating a CI/CD pipeline with GitHub Actions or Azure DevOps. A real-world example demonstrates deploying a portfolio website.

Preparing Your Application for Deployment

1. **Configuration Management**:
   o Use **appsettings.json** for environment-specific configurations (e.g., development, production).
   o Example of appsettings.Production.json:

   json

   ```
   {
     "ConnectionStrings": {
       "DefaultConnection":              "Server=prod-
       db;Database=MyApp;User
       Id=admin;Password=prodpassword;"
     }
   ```

```
}
```

2. **Environment Variables**:
   - Set sensitive information like API keys and connection strings using environment variables.
   - Example in Program.cs:

   csharp

   ```
   builder.Configuration.AddEnvironmentVariables();
   ```

3. **Build and Publish the Application**:
   - Build and publish the application for production:

   bash

   ```
   dotnet publish -c Release -o ./publish
   ```

4. **Enable HTTPS**:
   - Configure HTTPS redirection in Program.cs:

   csharp

   ```
   app.UseHttpsRedirection();
   ```

5. **Optimize Logging**:
   - Use structured logging and configure logging levels for production.

Deployment Options

1. **Azure (Microsoft Cloud Platform)**:
   o **App Service**:
     ▪ Ideal for hosting web applications.
     ▪ Steps:
         1. Create an App Service in the Azure portal.
         2. Deploy using the Azure CLI:

         bash

         az webapp up --name MyPortfolioApp --resource-group MyResourceGroup

         3. Configure settings like connection strings in the portal.
   o **Azure Kubernetes Service (AKS)**:
     ▪ For containerized applications requiring high scalability.
2. **AWS (Amazon Web Services)**:
   o **Elastic Beanstalk**:
     ▪ Simplifies application deployment.
     ▪ Steps:

1. Create an Elastic Beanstalk environment.

2. Deploy using the AWS CLI:

bash

```
eb init
eb deploy
```

o **Amazon EC2**:

▪ For custom deployment using virtual machines.

3. **On-Premises Servers**:

o Steps:

▪ Install .NET runtime on the server.

▪ Publish and copy files to the server.

▪ Configure the application with a reverse proxy like **Nginx** or **IIS**.

CI/CD Pipelines

1. **What Is CI/CD?**

o **Continuous Integration (CI)**: Automatically build and test code changes.

o **Continuous Deployment (CD)**: Automatically deploy code to production.

2. **GitHub Actions**:

- o Example Workflow:

yaml

```
name: Deploy to Azure
on:
  push:
    branches:
    - main
jobs:
  build-and-deploy:
    runs-on: ubuntu-latest
    steps:
    - name: Checkout code
      uses: actions/checkout@v3

    - name: Setup .NET
      uses: actions/setup-dotnet@v3
      with:
        dotnet-version: '6.0'

    - name: Build and publish
      run: |
        dotnet build --configuration Release
        dotnet publish -c Release -o publish

    - name: Deploy to Azure Web App
      uses: azure/webapps-deploy@v2
      with:
```

```yaml
          app-name: 'MyPortfolioApp'
          publish-profile:                    ${{
       secrets.AZURE_WEBAPP_PUBLISH_PROFILE }}
          package: ./publish
```

3. **Azure DevOps Pipelines**:
   o Example YAML Pipeline:

```yaml
yaml

trigger:
- main

pool:
  vmImage: 'ubuntu-latest'

steps:
- task: UseDotNet@2
  inputs:
    packageType: 'sdk'
    version: '6.x'

- script: dotnet build --configuration Release
  displayName: 'Build Project'

- script: dotnet publish -c Release -o
$(Build.ArtifactStagingDirectory)
  displayName: 'Publish Project'

- task: AzureWebApp@1
```

```
inputs:
    azureSubscription: 'AzureSubscription'
    appName: 'MyPortfolioApp'
    package: '$(Build.ArtifactStagingDirectory)'
```

Real-World Example: Deploying a Portfolio Website

Objective: Deploy a portfolio website using Azure App Service with CI/CD integration.

Step 1: Prepare the Application

1. Ensure the portfolio application is built using ASP.NET Core.
2. Add required settings in appsettings.json and appsettings.Production.json.

Step 2: Deploy Using Azure App Service

1. Install the Azure CLI:

bash

curl -sL https://aka.ms/InstallAzureCLIDeb | sudo bash

2. Log in to Azure:

bash

az login

3. Create an App Service:

bash

az webapp up --name MyPortfolioApp --runtime "DOTNET|6.0"

Step 3: Configure CI/CD with GitHub Actions

1. Add the GitHub Action workflow file
   to .github/workflows/deploy.yml:

yaml

name: Deploy to Azure

on:
  push:
    branches:
      - main

jobs:
  deploy:
    runs-on: ubuntu-latest

    steps:

```
- name: Checkout code
  uses: actions/checkout@v3

- name: Setup .NET
  uses: actions/setup-dotnet@v3
  with:
    dotnet-version: '6.0'

- name: Build and Publish
  run: |
    dotnet build --configuration Release
    dotnet publish -c Release -o ./publish

- name: Deploy to Azure Web App
  uses: azure/webapps-deploy@v2
  with:
    app-name: 'MyPortfolioApp'
    publish-profile:                           ${{
secrets.AZURE_WEBAPP_PUBLISH_PROFILE }}
    package: ./publish
```

2. Save and push the changes to the main branch.

Step 4: Verify Deployment

1. Access the portfolio website at
   https://MyPortfolioApp.azurewebsites.net.

2. Check the GitHub Actions workflow logs to ensure successful deployment.

In this chapter, you learned how to prepare an ASP.NET Core application for deployment, explored deployment options like Azure, AWS, and on-premises servers, and set up a CI/CD pipeline using GitHub Actions. The real-world example of deploying a portfolio website demonstrated these techniques in action. In the next chapter, we'll explore securing your application against common vulnerabilities.

Chapter 22: Real-Time Web Applications with SignalR

Real-time web applications enable seamless, bidirectional communication between servers and clients, allowing immediate updates without requiring client-side polling. In this chapter, you'll learn about SignalR, implement real-time notifications and updates, and build a real-world example of a live stock ticker.

Introduction to SignalR for Real-Time Communications

1. **What Is SignalR?**

    o   SignalR is a library for ASP.NET Core that facilitates real-time, bidirectional communication between clients and servers.

    o   It abstracts WebSockets, Server-Sent Events (SSE), and Long Polling, automatically choosing the best transport protocol based on the client and server capabilities.

2. **Why Use SignalR?**

    o   Real-time features such as live chat, notifications, and collaborative applications.

    o   Efficient server-to-client communication without frequent polling.

3. **How SignalR Works**:

   o Clients establish a persistent connection with the server.

   o The server pushes updates to all connected clients or specific groups of clients.

4. **SignalR Use Cases**:

   o Live stock tickers.

   o Chat applications.

   o Collaborative tools (e.g., real-time document editing).

   o Live notifications (e.g., sports scores, auction updates).

Implementing Real-Time Notifications and Updates

1. **Setting Up SignalR**:

   o Install the SignalR NuGet package:

   bash

   ```
   dotnet add package Microsoft.AspNetCore.SignalR
   ```

2. **Creating a SignalR Hub**:

   o A SignalR hub is a central communication point for clients and the server.

o Example: Define a StockHub for sending real-time stock updates:

csharp

```
using Microsoft.AspNetCore.SignalR;

public class StockHub : Hub
{
    public async Task SendStockUpdate(string stockSymbol,
decimal price)
    {
        await    Clients.All.SendAsync("ReceiveStockUpdate",
stockSymbol, price);
    }
}
```

3. **Configuring SignalR in Program.cs**:

o Register the SignalR hub and configure endpoints:

csharp

```
builder.Services.AddSignalR();
app.UseEndpoints(endpoints =>
{
    endpoints.MapHub<StockHub>("/stockHub");
});
```

4. **Connecting the Client**:

o Include the SignalR JavaScript library in the client:

html

```
<script src="https://cdnjs.cloudflare.com/ajax/libs/microsoft-signalr/5.0.13/signalr.min.js"></script>
```

o Establish a connection and handle updates:

html

```
<script>
  const connection = new signalR.HubConnectionBuilder().withUrl("/stockHub").build();

  connection.on("ReceiveStockUpdate", (stockSymbol, price) => {
    const stockRow = document.getElementById(stockSymbol);
    if (stockRow) {
      stockRow.textContent = `Price: $${price.toFixed(2)}`;
    } else {
      const row = document.createElement("div");
      row.id = stockSymbol;
      row.textContent = `${stockSymbol} - Price: $${price.toFixed(2)}`;

document.getElementById("stocks").appendChild(row);
    }
  });
```

```
connection.start().catch(err => console.error(err.toString()));
</script>
```

Real-World Example: Building a Live Stock Ticker

Objective: Create a live stock ticker application where clients receive real-time stock price updates.

Step 1: Define the Hub

1. Create a StockHub class:

csharp

```csharp
using Microsoft.AspNetCore.SignalR;

public class StockHub : Hub
{
    public async Task BroadcastStockPrice(string stockSymbol, decimal price)
    {
        await Clients.All.SendAsync("UpdateStockPrice", stockSymbol, price);
    }
}
```

Step 2: Configure SignalR

1. Register SignalR services and endpoints in Program.cs:

csharp

```
builder.Services.AddSignalR();
app.UseEndpoints(endpoints =>
{
    endpoints.MapHub<StockHub>("/stockHub");
});
```

Step 3: Create the Client Interface

1. Design the HTML interface:

html

```
<div>
    <h1>Live Stock Ticker</h1>
    <div id="stocks"></div>
</div>
<script src="https://cdnjs.cloudflare.com/ajax/libs/microsoft-signalr/5.0.13/signalr.min.js"></script>
<script>
    const connection = new signalR.HubConnectionBuilder().withUrl("/stockHub").build();

    connection.on("UpdateStockPrice", (stockSymbol, price) => {
        const stockDiv = document.getElementById(stockSymbol);
        if (stockDiv) {
```

```
        stockDiv.textContent        =        `${stockSymbol}:
$${price.toFixed(2)}`;
      } else {
        const newDiv = document.createElement("div");
        newDiv.id = stockSymbol;
        newDiv.textContent = `${stockSymbol}: $${price.toFixed(2)}`;
        document.getElementById("stocks").appendChild(newDiv);
      }
    });

    connection.start().catch(err => console.error(err.toString()));
  </script>
```

Step 4: Simulate Real-Time Updates

1. Create a service to simulate stock updates:

csharp

```csharp
public class StockService : BackgroundService
{
    private readonly IHubContext<StockHub> _hubContext;

    public StockService(IHubContext<StockHub> hubContext)
    {
        _hubContext = hubContext;
    }
```

```csharp
protected override async Task ExecuteAsync(CancellationToken
stoppingToken)
{
    var random = new Random();
    var stocks = new List<string> { "AAPL", "GOOGL", "MSFT",
"TSLA" };

    while (!stoppingToken.IsCancellationRequested)
    {
        foreach (var stock in stocks)
        {
            var price = random.Next(100, 1500) + random.NextDouble();
            await
_hubContext.Clients.All.SendAsync("UpdateStockPrice", stock, price);
            await Task.Delay(2000, stoppingToken);
        }
    }
}
```

2. Register the service in Program.cs:

csharp

```csharp
builder.Services.AddHostedService<StockService>();
```

Step 5: Run and Test

1. Start the application:

216

bash

dotnet run

2. Open the browser and navigate to the application.
3. Observe real-time updates as stock prices change every few seconds.

In this chapter, you learned about SignalR and how to implement real-time notifications and updates in ASP.NET Core. The real-world example of a live stock ticker demonstrated SignalR's ability to handle live updates seamlessly. These skills are valuable for creating modern, interactive web applications.

Chapter 23: Building Single-Page Applications with Blazor

Blazor is a framework for building interactive, client-side web applications using C#. It allows developers to create single-page applications (SPAs) without relying heavily on JavaScript. This chapter introduces Blazor, explores its integration with ASP.NET Core, and walks through a real-world example of building a SPA with Blazor.

Introduction to Blazor for C# Web Development

1. **What Is Blazor?**

   o Blazor is a .NET-based framework for building web UIs.

   o It supports two hosting models:

     ▪ **Blazor Server**: Runs on the server, and updates are sent to the client over SignalR.

     ▪ **Blazor WebAssembly**: Runs entirely on the client in the browser.

2. **Why Use Blazor?**

   o Write client-side logic in C#, eliminating the need for JavaScript for most use cases.

- o Reuse .NET libraries and share code between server and client.
- o Full-stack development with a single programming language.

3. **Blazor vs. Traditional SPAs**:
   - o While traditional SPAs like Angular, React, and Vue rely heavily on JavaScript, Blazor allows you to leverage your C# skills for front-end development.

Integrating Blazor with ASP.NET Core

1. **Setting Up a Blazor Project**:
   - o Create a Blazor WebAssembly project:

   bash

   ```
   dotnet new blazorwasm -o MyBlazorApp
   ```

   - o Or create a Blazor Server project:

   bash

   ```
   dotnet new blazorserver -o MyBlazorApp
   ```

2. **Adding Blazor to an ASP.NET Core Project**:
   - o Install the Blazor WebAssembly package:

bash

dotnet   add   package
Microsoft.AspNetCore.Components.WebAssembly.Server

o   Update Program.cs to configure Blazor:

csharp

builder.Services.AddRazorComponents(); // For Blazor Server

3. **Blazor File Structure**:

   o   **Pages**: Contains .razor files for each route.

   o   **Shared**: Contains shared components like headers or footers.

   o   **wwwroot**: Hosts static files like CSS and JavaScript.

4. **Adding Components**:

   o   Components are reusable UI elements defined in .razor files.

   o   Example:

razor

```
<h1>Hello, Blazor!</h1>

@code {
    private string message = "Welcome to Blazor!";
}
```

5. **Routing in Blazor**:

   o   Define routes using the @page directive:

   razor

   ```
   @page "/home"
   <h1>Home Page</h1>
   ```

Real-World Example: Building a SPA with Blazor

Objective: Build a simple SPA with Blazor to manage a task list.

Step 1: Create a New Blazor Server Project

1. Create the project:

   bash

   ```
   dotnet new blazorserver -o TaskManagerApp
   ```

2. Run the application:

   bash

   ```
   dotnet run
   ```

Step 2: Design the Task Model

1. Add a TaskItem class:

csharp

```csharp
public class TaskItem
{
    public int Id { get; set; }
    public string Title { get; set; }
    public bool IsCompleted { get; set; }
}
```

Step 3: Create a Task Management Component

1. Add a new component TaskList.razor in the Pages folder:

razor

```razor
@page "/tasks"
<h3>Task Manager</h3>

<input @bind="newTaskTitle" placeholder="New task..." />
<button @onclick="AddTask">Add Task</button>

<ul>
    @foreach (var task in tasks)
    {
        <li>
            <input type="checkbox" @bind="task.IsCompleted" />
            @task.Title
```

```
        </li>
    }
</ul>

@code {
    private List<TaskItem> tasks = new();
    private string newTaskTitle = string.Empty;

    private void AddTask()
    {
        if (!string.IsNullOrWhiteSpace(newTaskTitle))
        {
            tasks.Add(new TaskItem { Id = tasks.Count + 1, Title =
newTaskTitle });
            newTaskTitle = string.Empty;
        }
    }
}
```

Step 4: Add Navigation

1. Update Shared/NavMenu.razor to include a link to the task manager:

razor

```
<a href="/tasks" class="nav-link">Task Manager</a>
```

Step 5: Style the Application

1. Add custom styles in wwwroot/css/app.css:

css

```
body {
    font-family: Arial, sans-serif;
}

h3 {
    color: #4CAF50;
}

ul {
    list-style-type: none;
    padding: 0;
}

li {
    margin: 5px 0;
}

input[type="checkbox"] {
    margin-right: 10px;
}
```

2. Reference the CSS file in wwwroot/index.html or _Host.cshtml:

html

```
<link href="css/app.css" rel="stylesheet" />
```

Step 6: Test the Application

1. Run the application:

    bash

    dotnet run

2. Navigate to /tasks and test the task manager functionality.

In this chapter, you explored the basics of Blazor for building SPAs and learned how to integrate Blazor with ASP.NET Core. The real-world example of a task manager demonstrated how to create and manage components, implement routing, and bind data in Blazor. These skills are foundational for building rich, interactive web applications with C#.

Chapter 24: Security Best Practices

Security is a critical aspect of web application development. This chapter covers best practices for protecting your ASP.NET Core applications from common threats, such as SQL injection, cross-site scripting (XSS), and cross-site request forgery (CSRF). You'll also learn about securing sensitive data with HTTPS and encryption. Finally, a real-world example demonstrates implementing OAuth for third-party authentication.

Protecting Your Application from Common Threats

1. **SQL Injection**:
   - SQL injection occurs when attackers inject malicious SQL code into queries, potentially compromising the database.

   Best Practices:

   - Use parameterized queries:

   csharp

   ```
   var command = new SqlCommand("SELECT * FROM Users
   WHERE Username = @username", connection);
   ```

```
command.Parameters.AddWithValue("@username",
username);
```

- o Use an Object-Relational Mapper (ORM) like **Entity Framework**, which handles parameterized queries automatically:

csharp

```
var user = dbContext.Users.FirstOrDefault(u => u.Username
== username);
```

2. **Cross-Site Scripting (XSS)**:

- o XSS attacks inject malicious scripts into web pages viewed by other users.

Best Practices:

- o Always encode output to prevent malicious scripts from executing:

html

```html
<span>@Html.Encode(userInput)</span>
```

- o Use Razor's built-in encoding for dynamic content:

razor

```razor
<div>@userInput</div>
```

3. **Cross-Site Request Forgery (CSRF)**:

   o CSRF attacks trick users into performing actions they didn't intend, like submitting forms.

Best Practices:

   o Use ASP.NET Core's built-in anti-CSRF features:

   html

   ```html
   <form method="post">
     <input type="hidden" name="__RequestVerificationToken" value="@AntiForgeryToken()" />
   </form>
   ```

   o Ensure the ValidateAntiForgeryToken attribute is applied to controller actions:

   csharp

   ```csharp
   [HttpPost]
   [ValidateAntiForgeryToken]
   public IActionResult SubmitForm(Model model)
   {
       // Action logic
   }
   ```

Using HTTPS and Securing Sensitive Data

1. **Enable HTTPS**:
   - o HTTPS encrypts communication between the client and server.
   - o Redirect all HTTP traffic to HTTPS:

   csharp

   ```
   app.UseHttpsRedirection();
   ```

2. **Protect Sensitive Data**:
   - o Store sensitive data, like connection strings and API keys, securely in environment variables or secrets:

   bash

   ```
   export
   ConnectionStrings__Default="Server=myServer;Database=myDB;User Id=myUser;Password=myPass;"
   ```

   - o Access them in your application:

   csharp

   ```
   var                    connectionString              =
   builder.Configuration.GetConnectionString("Default");
   ```

3. **Use Data Protection API**:
   - o Encrypt sensitive data using ASP.NET Core's Data Protection API:

```
csharp

var                     protector                =
dataProtectionProvider.CreateProtector("MyApp.Purpose");
var encryptedData = protector.Protect("SensitiveData");
var decryptedData = protector.Unprotect(encryptedData);
```

Real-World Example: Implementing OAuth for Third-Party Authentication

OAuth is an open standard for secure authentication, allowing users to log in using third-party services like Google, Facebook, or GitHub.

Objective: Implement Google OAuth authentication in an ASP.NET Core application.

Step 1: Register the Application with Google

1. Go to the Google Cloud Console.
2. Create a new project and enable the **Google+ API**.
3. Configure OAuth consent screen.
4. Generate OAuth client credentials.
   - **Client ID** and **Client Secret** will be provided.

Step 2: Configure OAuth in ASP.NET Core

1. Add the required NuGet package:

bash

dotnet add package Microsoft.AspNetCore.Authentication.Google

2. Configure authentication in Program.cs:

csharp

```
builder.Services.AddAuthentication(options =>
{
    options.DefaultAuthenticateScheme           =
CookieAuthenticationDefaults.AuthenticationScheme;
    options.DefaultChallengeScheme              =
GoogleDefaults.AuthenticationScheme;
})
.AddCookie()
.AddGoogle(options =>
{
    options.ClientId = "YourGoogleClientID";
    options.ClientSecret = "YourGoogleClientSecret";
});

app.UseAuthentication();
app.UseAuthorization();
```

3. Protect a controller action:

csharp

```
[Authorize]
public class AccountController : Controller
{
    public IActionResult Login()
    {
        return Challenge(new AuthenticationProperties { RedirectUri = "/"
}, GoogleDefaults.AuthenticationScheme);
    }

    public IActionResult Logout()
    {
        HttpContext.SignOutAsync();
        return Redirect("/");
    }
}
```

Step 3: Create the Login and Logout Links

1. Add links in your layout file (_Layout.cshtml or equivalent):

html

```
@if (User.Identity.IsAuthenticated)
{
    <a asp-controller="Account" asp-action="Logout">Logout</a>
}
else
{
```

```
<a  asp-controller="Account"  asp-action="Login">Login  with
Google</a>
}
```

Step 4: Test Authentication

1. Run the application:

   bash

   dotnet run

2. Click the "Login with Google" link and log in using your Google account.
3. Verify the authentication status and user details.

In this chapter, you learned security best practices for protecting ASP.NET Core applications from common threats like SQL injection, XSS, and CSRF. You explored how to secure sensitive data with HTTPS and encryption and implemented OAuth for third-party authentication using Google as an example. These techniques help ensure your applications are secure and robust against modern threats.

Chapter 25: Scaling Your Application

Scaling ensures your ASP.NET Core application can handle high traffic and growing user demands without degrading performance. This chapter explores techniques for scaling, including using load balancers, implementing auto-scaling groups, and designing your application for scalability. A real-world example of scaling an online event registration system demonstrates these concepts in action.

Scaling ASP.NET Core Applications for High Traffic

1. **What Is Scaling?**
   - **Vertical Scaling (Scale-Up)**: Increases the capacity of a single server by adding resources (CPU, RAM, etc.).
   - **Horizontal Scaling (Scale-Out)**: Adds more servers to distribute the load across multiple instances.
2. **Best Practices for Scalability**:
   - **Stateless Architecture**:
     - Store session data in distributed caches like Redis instead of server memory.
   - **Database Optimization**:
     - Use read replicas for read-heavy applications.

- Implement sharding for large datasets.
  - **Asynchronous Processing**:
    - Offload long-running tasks to background workers or message queues.
  - **Caching**:
    - Cache frequently accessed data in memory or distributed caches.
  - **CDN for Static Content**:
    - Serve images, CSS, and JavaScript files through a Content Delivery Network (CDN).

3. **ASP.NET Core Features for Scaling**:
   - **Response Caching**:
     - Reduces the load by serving cached responses.
   - **Distributed Caching**:
     - Use tools like Redis or SQL Server for shared caching across servers.
   - **Health Checks**:
     - Monitor application health to ensure only healthy instances serve traffic.

Using Load Balancers and Auto-Scaling Groups

1. **Load Balancers**:

- o Distribute incoming traffic across multiple servers to ensure no single server is overwhelmed.

- o Common Load Balancer Options:

  - **AWS Elastic Load Balancer (ELB)**.

  - **Azure Load Balancer**.

  - **NGINX or HAProxy** for on-premises setups.

2. **Auto-Scaling Groups**:

  - o Automatically adjust the number of instances based on traffic.

  - o Common Platforms:

    - **AWS Auto Scaling**.

    - **Azure Virtual Machine Scale Sets**.

3. **Session Management with Load Balancers**:

  - o Use sticky sessions sparingly.

  - o Prefer distributed session management (e.g., Redis or database).

4. **Configuring Load Balancers**:

  - o AWS Example:

    - Create a target group and attach your instances.

    - Configure a listener for HTTP or HTTPS traffic.

  - o Azure Example:

    - Use **Azure Traffic Manager** to route traffic intelligently.

Real-World Example: Scaling an Online Event Registration System

Objective: Scale an online event registration system to handle high traffic during ticket sales.

Step 1: Design a Scalable Architecture

1. **Stateless Application**:
   - Store session data in a distributed cache (e.g., Redis).
   - Store uploaded files in a scalable storage solution like AWS S3 or Azure Blob Storage.
2. **Database Optimization**:
   - Use a primary database for writes and read replicas for queries.
   - Enable connection pooling for efficient database connections.

Step 2: Implement Distributed Caching

1. Add Redis caching to the application:

bash

```
dotnet add package Microsoft.Extensions.Caching.StackExchangeRedis
```

2. Configure Redis in Program.cs:

csharp

```csharp
builder.Services.AddStackExchangeRedisCache(options =>
{
    options.Configuration = "localhost:6379"; // Replace with your Redis
connection string
});
```

3. Use Redis to cache popular event data:

csharp

```csharp
public class EventService
{
    private readonly IDistributedCache _cache;

    public EventService(IDistributedCache cache)
    {
        _cache = cache;
    }

    public async Task<string> GetEventDetailsAsync(string eventId)
    {
        var cacheKey = $"Event_{eventId}";
        var cachedData = await _cache.GetStringAsync(cacheKey);

        if (cachedData != null)
```

```
    {
        return cachedData;
    }

    // Simulate fetching event details from the database
    var eventData = $"Details for event {eventId}";
    await    _cache.SetStringAsync(cacheKey,    eventData,    new
DistributedCacheEntryOptions
    {
        AbsoluteExpirationRelativeToNow                =
TimeSpan.FromMinutes(10)
    });

    return eventData;
    }
}
```

Step 3: Add Load Balancing

1. Deploy the application to multiple instances:

   o Use **AWS EC2** or **Azure Virtual Machines**.

2. Configure a load balancer:

   o AWS ELB Example:

     ▪ Create an ELB and register your instances.

     ▪ Set health check paths to /health.

   o Azure Example:

     ▪ Create an Azure Load Balancer and add your
       virtual machines to a backend pool.

3. Verify load balancing:

    o Use tools like **Apache JMeter** or **Locust** to simulate traffic and monitor server utilization.

Step 4: Configure Auto-Scaling

1. AWS Auto Scaling Example:

    o Create an auto-scaling group linked to your load balancer.

    o Set scaling policies:

       ▪ Scale out when CPU utilization exceeds 70%.

       ▪ Scale in when CPU utilization drops below 30%.

2. Azure Virtual Machine Scale Sets:

    o Configure auto-scaling rules based on metrics like CPU or memory usage.

Step 5: Monitor Performance

1. Use monitoring tools to ensure optimal performance:

    o AWS: **CloudWatch**.

    o Azure: **Application Insights**.

2. Implement health checks:

    o Add health check endpoints in your application:

csharp

```
builder.Services.AddHealthChecks();
app.UseHealthChecks("/health");
```

Step 6: Test Scalability

1. Simulate peak traffic using **JMeter** or **Locust**.
2. Monitor the application's response time, error rate, and server utilization during the test.

In this chapter, you learned how to scale ASP.NET Core applications for high traffic, use load balancers and auto-scaling groups, and implement distributed caching. The real-world example of scaling an online event registration system demonstrated practical steps to handle high traffic scenarios effectively.

Chapter 26: Wrapping It Up

Congratulations on reaching the end of this comprehensive journey into C# for web development with ASP.NET Core! This chapter recaps the key concepts and technologies covered, suggests real-world project ideas for further practice, and provides pathways for continued learning and certification to deepen your expertise.

Recap of Key Concepts and Technologies

1. **Core C# Concepts**:
   - Variables, data types, control structures, and object-oriented programming.
   - Asynchronous programming with async and await.

2. **ASP.NET Core Fundamentals**:
   - MVC architecture (Model-View-Controller).
   - Razor Pages and Blazor for building interactive UIs.
   - Dependency Injection (DI) and middleware for modular and extensible applications.

3. **APIs and Real-Time Applications**:
   - Building RESTful APIs and using GraphQL for flexible queries.
   - Real-time communication with SignalR.

4. **Security Best Practices**:

o Protecting against SQL injection, XSS, and CSRF attacks.

o Implementing OAuth for third-party authentication.

5. **Performance Optimization**:

o Caching, compression, and bundling techniques.

o Scaling applications with load balancers and auto-scaling groups.

6. **Deployment**:

o Deploying applications to cloud platforms like Azure and AWS.

o Setting up CI/CD pipelines for automated builds and deployments.

Real-World Project Ideas for Practice

1. **E-Commerce Platform**:

o Features:

▪ Product catalog and filtering.

▪ User authentication and roles (admin, user).

▪ Shopping cart and order processing.

o Technologies:

▪ ASP.NET Core MVC, Entity Framework, and SignalR for real-time notifications.

2. **Blog or Content Management System (CMS)**:

- o Features:
    - Rich text editor for post creation.
    - Role-based content management.
    - API for mobile integration.
- o Technologies:
    - ASP.NET Core Razor Pages, Blazor, and GraphQL.

3. **Real-Time Chat Application**:
   - o Features:
       - Private and group chat.
       - User presence detection.
       - File sharing.
   - o Technologies:
       - SignalR, Redis for caching, and WebSockets for real-time updates.

4. **Online Learning Platform**:
   - o Features:
       - Course catalog, enrollment, and progress tracking.
       - Video streaming integration.
       - Quizzes and assignments.
   - o Technologies:
       - Blazor WebAssembly, APIs, and Azure Blob Storage for video hosting.

5. **Task Management System**:

- o Features:
  - Drag-and-drop task management.
  - Notifications for due dates.
  - Multi-user collaboration.
- o Technologies:
  - Blazor Server, SignalR, and distributed caching.

Pathways for Continued Learning

1. **Advanced Topics**:
   - o **Cloud Development**: Learn Azure or AWS for cloud-native applications.
   - o **Microservices Architecture**: Explore Kubernetes, Docker, and Dapr for microservices.
   - o **Machine Learning**: Use ML.NET or integrate external machine learning models.
2. **Certifications**:
   - o **Microsoft Certified: Azure Developer Associate**:
     - Covers Azure fundamentals and application deployment.
   - o **AWS Certified Developer - Associate**:
     - Focuses on developing cloud applications with AWS.

- o **Microsoft Certified: C# Specialist** (optional but beneficial).

3. **Open Source Contributions**:
   - o Contribute to ASP.NET Core or other C# projects on GitHub.
   - o Collaborate with the community to learn best practices.

4. **Stay Updated**:
   - o Follow Microsoft's ASP.NET Blog.
   - o Attend .NET and web development conferences or webinars.

You've now built a strong foundation in C# for web development and gained hands-on experience with ASP.NET Core. Whether you're creating APIs, real-time applications, or scalable systems, the knowledge and skills from this book position you for success in modern web development.

As you move forward, remember:

- **Practice consistently**: Real-world projects are the best way to learn.
- **Stay curious**: Technology evolves, so keep exploring new tools and trends.

- **Share your knowledge**: Teaching others is a great way to reinforce your understanding.

The world of C# and ASP.NET Core is vast and exciting—your journey has just begun. Happy coding!

www.ingramcontent.com/pod-product-compliance
Lightning Source LLC
Chambersburg PA
CBHW070941050326
40689CB00014B/3296